VATICAN II AND THE
ECUMENICAL WAY

GEORGE H. TAVARD

VATICAN II AND THE
ECUMENICAL WAY

MARQUETTE
UNIVERSITY
PRESS

Marquette Studies in Theology
No. 52
Andrew Tallon, Series Editor

Library of Congress Cataloging-in-Publication Data

Tavard, George H. (George Henry), 1922-
Vatican II and the ecumenical way / George H. Tavard.
    p. cm. — (Marquette studies in theology ; no. 52)
Includes bibliographical references and index.
ISBN-13: 978-0-87462-729-9 (pbk. : alk. paper)
ISBN-10: 0-87462-729-X (pbk. : alk. paper)
1. Vatican Council (2nd : 1962-1965) 2. Vatican Council (2nd : 1962-1965).
Decretum de oecumenismo. 3. Christian union--Catholic Church. I. Title.
BX8301962 .T38 2007
262.001'1—dc22

                                                                    2006033789

Cover photo by Andrew J. Tallon

♾The paper used in this publication meets the minimum requirements of the
American National Standard for Information Sciences—
Permanence of Paper for Printed Library Materials, ANSI Z39.48-1992.

Association of American
University Presses

MARQUETTE UNIVERSITY PRESS
MILWAUKEE

The Association of Jesuit University Presses

CONTENTS

FOREWORD

The present volume is the fruit of my experience and my reflections, since Vatican Council II, on the general theme of the ecumenical dialogue and its method. When Pope John XXIII created the Secretariat for the Promotion of Christian Unity he named me a consultant. Two years later he appointed me to the Vatican Council itself as a conciliar *peritus*. At the end of the council I was named to several of the ecumenical dialogues that started in the next few years. Internationally I worked in the preliminary commission that composed the *Malta Report*, then in the Anglican-Roman Catholic Conversations (ARCIC-I) that composed the *Final Report*. After ARCIC-I I closed in 1981 I was appointed to the international dialogue of the Catholic Church with the World Methodist Council. In the United States I have taken part in the dialogues with the Episcopal Church and with the Lutheran Churches since both of them started in 1965.

I have published a number of essays on Vatican II that are not included in this volume, notably: *Dogmatic Constitution on Divine Revelation of Vatican Council II. Commentary and translation* (Glen Rock, NJ: Paulist Press, 1966); "Praying Together. *Communicatio in sacris* in the decree on *ecumenism*" (Alberic Stacpoole, *Vatican II by those who were there*, London: Geoffrey Chapman, 1986, p. 202-219), "Ecumenical Relations" (Adrian Hastings, ed., *Modern Catholicism. Vatican II and After*, London; SPCK, 1991, p. 398-421); "Vatican II, Understood and Misunderstood" (*One in Christ*, 1991/3, p.209-221); "Commentary on the decree on ecumenism" (Vincent A. Yzermans, ed., *American Participation in the Second Vatican Council*, New York: Sheed and Ward, 1997, p. 321-334; "Reminiscences and Lessons from an Ecumenical Journey" (*The Jurist*, 58/1, 1998, p. 198-212); "American Contributions to Vatican II's Documents on Ecumenism and on Religious Liberty" (*Chicago Studies*, Spring 2003, vol. 21/1, p. 17-30); "The Decree on Ecumenism. Forty Years later" (*Ecumenism*, 40th Year, n. 157/158. March/June 2005, Montreal, P. Q., p.5-19). Several other lectures have not been published. The following pages reproduce some of these papers and lectures, or amalgamate data from several of them. In most cases the material has been reworked and some of it extensively rewritten.

After a historical introduction chapter 1 will describe my ecumenical itinerary. I will then pay special attention to Vatican Council II and the decree on Ecumenism (chapter 2). I will next reflect on the theology of dialogue (chapter 3) and insist on the necessity to develop a theological language across the diverse Christian traditions (chapters 4 and 5). This will lead to further reflection on ecclesiology in ecumenical perspective (chapters 6 and 7), and on the general question of the reception of ecumenical agreements (chapter 8). A conclusion will sum up some of the lessons that emerge from the Church's ecumenical commitment. An appendix will face a question which, though not immediately ecumenical, opens a perspective on the growing dialogue between all major religions: "Can theology be nonverbal?"

I wish these pages to be a testimony to the ecumenical vision of Pope John XXIII, of Cardinal Augustine Bea, and of Cardinal Jan Willebrands, thanks to whose enlightened and gentle leadership the Catholic Church officially entered the ecumenical movement and initiated remarkable progress toward the reconciliation of divided Christians. I also wish to express my gratitude to the Sisters of Mercy of Pittsburgh, and to the Faculty and students of Mount Mercy College in Pittsburgh (now Carlow University), where I chaired the Department of Theology when Pope John called me to the council. All of them willingly cooperated in making my absence tolerable during the Fall of four successive years. In partial reward for their assistance, I always gave a report to the College when I returned from each session. Mount Mercy-Carlow was probably the best-informed liberal arts college of women in the United States in regard to the happenings at Vatican Council II and their meaning for the future of the Church.

The early historian Eusebius reported that Papias looked for witnesses who had known some direct disciples of the Apostles. "Because," Papias explained, "I did not think that books could be as helpful to me as what comes from a living and lasting voice." Although the present volume is a book, it is, forty years after the events, the record of a living, if not lasting, voice.

George H. Tavard
Assumption Center
Brighton, MA

INTRODUCTION

THE WAY TO VATICAN II

The impression is sometimes given that Pope John XXIII's conciliar project appeared all of a sudden, an unexpected shooting star in a dark sky. If this were the case, the declarations, decrees, and constitutions of the council would stand by themselves, unconnected, except by opposition, with whatever preceded the council. Then the council could also remain unconnected with its aftermath, a surd without a past or a future. In reality Vatican II followed the clash of two trends in ecclesiology, and was the logical outcome of one of them. A brief review of the first half of the twentieth century throws light on this aspect of Vatican II and its implications.

Politically the twentieth century opened in Europe on a dark series for the Catholic Church. It started in France in the middle of the Dreyfus affair. Alfred Dreyfus (1859-1935), a Jewish officer in the French army, had been condemned for high treason, as an alleged spy working for Germany, in 1896. He was to be rehabilitated in 1906. This was both a case of erroneous judgment and harsh sentencing by a military court, and a case of anti-Semitism in public opinion. But it was also much more. French Catholics were divided on the matter of Dreyfus's guilt or innocence. The great poet Charles Péguy (1873-1914) strenuously defended his innocence. But many in the clergy and most of the official and unofficial Catholic Press were somehow convinced of his guilt. There were long sequels. Still in 1938, a Catholic periodical, published in Paris by the community to which I belong, approved the following statement: "Anti-Semitism, as it was taught by St. Thomas Aquinas and practiced by the popes, should be, in the measure that is allowed by the present conditions of society, the program of all Christian countries."[1] In 1928, Pius XI condemned Les Amis d'Israel, an association founded two years

---

1. Quoted (in a critical perspective) in a commemorative issue: *La Documentation Catholique*, n. 2000, vol. LXXXVII, 18 February 1990, n. 4, p. 213.

before to fight anti-Semitism among Catholics. It advocated avoiding to speak of a deicide people or of the conversion of Jews," thus anticipating measures that Vatican II adopted. Nine years later, the same pope declared to a group of Belgian pilgrims, "Spiritually, we are Semites," and he condemned the anti-Semitism of the Nazis in the encyclical Mit brennender Sorge. This illustrates the ups and downs of a quasi-official anti-Semitism. It also raises a directly ecclesiological question: What is the Church's self-understanding in regard to its Jewish origin?

Undoubtedly, the ecclesiology of the first half of the twentieth century was affected by the political problems of Europe. In France the Third Republic had, in 1905, unilaterally repudiated the concordat passed in 1801 between Napoleon and Pius VII. At the same time all religious devoted to education were forbidden to teach, all Church property was nationalized, and social privileges of the clergy were abolished. Catholics in the German Empire also suffered severe discrimination under the impact of Bismarck's Kulturkampf, which regarded Catholicism as a foreign, non Teutonic religion. In Italy, the popes, faithful to the policy of Pius IX (1846-1878), remained "prisoners in the Vatican," refusing to give up their medieval temporal authority and to recognize the annexation of the Papal States to the kingdom of Italy. In 1870, Pio Nono had proclaimed the doctrine of papal infallibility largely as a challenge to the modern world, in the spirit of his list of errors, the Syllabus, of 1864. Leo XIII (1878-1903) had made openings toward better relations with both the French Republic and the people of England,[2] but he gave up trying to make peace with an Italy that was not willing to reach a compromise about the Papal States. The Church was caught as it was between the aggressiveness of the ones and the intransigence of the others.

Doctrinally, the nineteenth century had ended with the condemnation of Americanism, precisely by Leo XIII (encyclical *Testem benevolentiae*, January 1899). Whether it was actually professed or not, the "phantom heresy" was directly ecclesiological. For it assumed that humanity can, with the grace of God, bring about the Kingdom. And, not unlike the Mormons, it suggested that the Kingdom was likely to come about on the

2. Apostolic letter *Au milieu des sollicitudes* (February 1892), addressed to the French bishops; letter *Notre consolation* (March 1892), to the French cardinals; apostolic letter *Amantissimae voluntatis* (April 1895), addressed *ad anglos*.

banks of the Great Lakes and the valley of the Mississippi[3]. It would take the form of political democracy. It would strive on the supremacy of the English language, the exclusive reign of the Latin liturgy, capitalist enterprise, and the magic of the market. In other words, it was a new and virulent form of Pelagianism, set, however, in the area of politics no less than in that of the spiritual life.

As the twentieth century inherited the mood of the nineteenth, such ideas were given a new context by the more intellectual and academic conceptions of Modernism. Although the Catholic forms of Modernism espoused no specific plan for the Church, the view of Alfred Loisy was typical: "Jesus foretold the Kingdom, and it was the Church that came." In other words, the Church, as an institution that would last through the centuries, was unforeseen by Jesus. Any claim, of the Church, of the papacy, or even of the sacraments, to have been founded by him could only be taken in a symbolic sense. Pius X (1903-1914) feared that such a spiritual symbolism of Christian origins undermined the Catholic conception of the Church, and he condemned it in 1907, in the decree *Lamentabili* and the encyclical *Pascendi*. But Pius X, or at least some members of the Roman curia, went further. In the form of the *Societas Pii Noni* (SPN, whence the French nickname, la Sapinière, the "Fir tree Nursery"), a secret society fought Modernism through denunciations and innuendos. Catholic ecclesiology took a peculiar orientation: the Church should be aggressively protected. This Counterreformation ecclesiology, inspired by Cardinal Bellarmine in the seventeenth century, was generally professed in the Roman schools and in the neo-scholasticism that had been promoted by Leo XIII. But it was more than a relic of the past. When Benedict XV (1914-1922) disbanded the *Societas Pii Noni*, its central presupposition remained: the Catholic institution constitutes an integral whole. It demands total adhesion to all details of Roman theology. It is threatened by rival or parallel theologies that may grow in other intellectual centers.

Following Vatican Council I, the codification of canon law, never before attempted, originated in a certain conception of the Church, which was then embodied in law. The code itself, promulgated in 1917, by Benedict XV, resulted from several decades of painstaking work. Now, the very notion of such a codification reflected a secular influence on the Church. It was inspired by the codification of French law by Napoleon, which itself was part of the Emperor's attempt to

3. See my volume, *Catholicism, USA*, New York: Newman Press, 1969.

reorganize the country after the chaos of the Great Revolution, but on the principle of centralization that was central to the legislative work of the Revolution. The code of 1917 accepted the Counterreformation thesis that the Church is a "perfect society," that is, "perfect in its kind and by right," as Leo XIII had written[4]. Now a perfect society should have a perfect legal system. In the system that was embodied in the code, the Church is in fact highly clerical. No section is devoted to the laity, which appears in it incidentally, in connection with the tasks of the clergy: the lay faithful are receivers of the sacraments and possible candidates for ordination, for interdict and excommunication, and eventually for canonization.

When Benedict XV created the Congregation for the Oriental Church, hitherto a desk in the Holy Office, and the Oriental Institute for the study and teaching of the Oriental rites and theologies, he placed the catholicity of the Church in a new light. Yet this light from the East was itself hesitant. The catholicity that it illustrated could de-emphasize the Western character of the Church and subordinate the Latin Church, headed by the bishop of Rome as patriarch of the West, to the Catholic Church, presided over by the bishop of Rome as successor of Peter. But it also could accentuate the "uniate" status of the Oriental Churches, and their subordination to the Latin Church, Latinity or Romanity being erroneously identified with catholicity. This identification seemed to prevail in Roman circles, at times coexisting with a real sense of universality.

The age of Pius XI (1922-1939) was nonetheless a time of Catholic revival. The creation of "catholic action," defined as a participation of the laity in the apostolate of the hierarchy, aimed, in the long run, at a renewal of parish life, of catechetical methods, and at a renewed evangelization of the modern world. Under the guidance of the Belgian Canon Joseph Cardijn (1882-1967), Catholic Action, in the form of la JOC, hoped to change the environment and the work conditions of the European working class. The transformation of the structures of society was viewed as an aspect, and even as a condition, of preaching the gospel in both its personal and its social dimensions. This was accompanied by a literary, intellectual, and spiritual awakening, which at

---

4. ... *societas ... genere et jure perfecta* (Encyclical *Immortale Dei*, 1885).

last began to renovate theological teaching after the difficult years of the repression of Modernism.

Pius XI finally gave up the secular claims of the popes to their medieval sovereignty over parts of Italy (the Papal States), and he abandoned the papacy's hostility to the Italian state and monarchy. The Lateran treatise, passed with Mussolini in 1929, accepted the shrinking of papal sovereignty to the City of the Vatican. Drawing the papacy away from secular political responsibilities, the treatise freed the bishop of Rome for greater catholicity and deeper spiritual influence, which the popes have tried to wield through frequent encyclicals and innumerable speeches. Pius XI also turned his attention to another aspect of the catholicity of the Church when he opened wide the Catholic priesthood to Asians and Africans, and he began the transfer of the episcopate in mission lands to native bishops.

The long pontificate of Pius XII (1939-1958) was highly ambiguous for the self-understanding of the Catholic Church. On the one hand, the pope had to struggle with the tragedies of the Second World War. This gave him many opportunities to speak and work in favor of international peace and of social justice. Most of his Christmas messages and many other addresses were in fact devoted to this political aspect of catholicity. As the situation evolved after the war, the pope's writings renewed with the tradition of Leo XIII and Pius XI in their analysis and condemnation of the technological society, both in its original form of capitalism and in its derived form of communism. As social involvement demanded the collaboration of all, believers and unbelievers alike, in the context of human society, it tended to open windows in the Catholic mind. The Church could no longer think of itself as a fortress against the world.

This openness was manifest in a series of doctrinal encyclicals. *Afflante Spiritu* (1943) endorsed scientific exegesis as a valid method for studying the Scriptures. *Mystici corporis* (1943) turned official Catholic ecclesiology toward the image of the Mystical Body, yet without modifying the central conceptions of the Counterreformation. It strictly identified the Roman Catholic institution and the Mystical Body of Christ, thus entailing a confusion of the political and the spiritual dimensions of the Church, and implying the exegetically and historically absurd thesis that Jesus of Nazareth himself did found the Church in its Roman Catholic form. *Mediator Dei* (1947) went back to the spiritual aspect of the Church, as it promoted the aims of the liturgical movement, and it was followed by the initiation of liturgical reform, in 1947 in regard to the "form" of the sacrament of orders, in 1955 regarding the ritual of Holy Week, and in 1957 in the matter of Eucharistic fast.

Meanwhile, however, Pius XII's practice of ecclesiology had not budged from the harsher conceptions of the Counterreformation. The dogmatic definition of Mary's Assumption into heaven (1950) reflected the pope's determination that neither the dogmatic development of doctrine nor the exercise of papal authority be hampered by the liberal democratic ideals that were abroad in the contemporary world. It also reflected the pope's disregard of Protestant theologians and Churches and of the ecumenical movement. In the same year 1950, the encyclical *Humani generis* purported to warn theologians against dangerous deviations from the Catholic line. Modern theology outside of Rome was more biblical and patristic than scholastic. It tried to learn from scientific research and theory in regard to the origins of humanity and of the cosmos. It accepted the turn to the subject, which is characteristic of the main currents in modern philosophy, and the consequent inevitability of toning down the objective concerns of St. Thomas, and of giving a greater place to historicity in Christian anthropology. Such a theological orientation undermined the very nature of neo-scholasticism, which since Leo XIII had been the official theology of the Holy See and the basis of theological education.

Pius XII, however, was little inclined to appreciate the value of initiatives that did not originate in Rome or were unsupported by the only theology he knew, neo-scholastic theology. Being himself more a diplomat and a canonist than a theologian, he followed a neo-scholasticism that was already obsolete in most theological centers outside of Rome. And the high-handed measures taken against several major theologians, who were silenced, and even, as in the case of Yves Congar, assigned to a specific residence, derived from Pius XII's basic indifference to theological research. It was in the same spirit that the priest-worker movement was discontinued. Initiated in 1945 by Cardinal Suhard, archbishop of Paris, in order to provide chaplains to young Frenchmen who were forcibly incorporated in the working force of the Third Reich at war, the worker-priest movement had survived the war in a new form. Worker-priests were to be the foci of a Christian presence in a dechristianized working class that was manipulated by the Communist Party. In 1955, Pius XII imposed strict limits to the activities of worker-priests, which made the continuation of the movement practically impossible. His decision was the token of a deeper and wider problem. Anyone who studied the theological situation between 1945 and 1959 could easily detect a growing discrepancy between the official trend of the papacy and the movements in Catholic thought that showed the greatest promise of creativity. In the last years of Pius XII the time was ripe for a change. "There came a man whose name was John."

In regard to the ecumenical movement the perspective was not entirely closed. The reticence of Benedict XV and Pius XI were set aside by Pius XII through the instruction of the Holy Office, *Ecclesia catholica* (20 September, 1949). In 1960 and 61, however, one could remember the failure of the Catholic Church to take advantage of the plenary meeting of the World Council of Churches in Evanston in 1959. The regulations of Pius XII had made each bishop responsible for all ecumenical gatherings in his diocese. When the World Council of Churches held its second plenary meeting in Evanston, the archbishop of Chicago, Cardinal Stritch, forbade Catholics to attend the gathering. It so happened that two theologians, a Benedictine from Belgium and a Dominican from France, had left Europe before the archbishop formulated his position. They paid him a visit, but he refused to authorize the exception they asked for. The only Catholics present came as journalists, on the assumption that the negative decision was not intended to leave the Catholic press without direct information. There clearly was a defect in a discipline that allowed an international opportunity to fail for purely local reasons.

To his lasting merit, John XXIII (1959-1963) perceived this discrepancy. And he began to close the gap. The council that he called was to be both a means to slow down the increasing irrelevancy of the papacy and therefore of the Church to the world at large, as well as an instrument to unify the laity and the hierarchy in a new vision of the Catholic purpose. The word, aggiornamento, which the pope chose to express his general intent, was vague enough to accommodate the two perspectives of internal reform and external reorientation. But one should not exaggerate the novelty of the pope's conciliar project. Papa Giovanni was himself a product of the conservative peasantry, of seminaries that were molded on the pattern of the Counter-reformation, and of an ecclesiastical career at the service of papal power. He wished to renovate the system, not to demolish it, to update it, not to undermine it. One day during the first session of the council, as the two of us were walking in the side aisle of St. Peter's basilica during one of the morning sessions, the future Cardinal Wright, then bishop of Pittsburgh, said to me: "I have the uneasy feeling that Pope John called this council in order to do what he had the power, but not the heart, to do..." The pope had the power to reform the Roman curia, but not the heart to fight its well-entrenched officers. The council was to be the pope's instrument to update the curia in general and the Holy Office in particular.

It must have been clear to Pope John that several lines of thought, that were alive outside of Rome, would be represented among the bishops of the world, and that they would clash during the council. The ultramontane line received new strength from Pius XII, and it was far from spent in Italy, geographically close to Rome, and in Spain, traditionally at home in a centralized system of government. It was still generally favored in Anglo-Saxon countries, nurtured by old distrusts of anything that sounded Protestant. In addition, the bishops of Communist countries could be expected to be wary of novelties, because turmoil and change in the Catholic community were the last thing that they wished on their hard-pressed people. The other main line of thought was alive among the French bishops. Most of the prominent theologians who incurred the disfavor of Pius XII were French. And the tradition of relative Gallican independence, that had been driven underground by Vatican Council I, was far from dead, even though no one now professed the central thesis of conciliarism on the supremacy of the council over the pope. The predominant influence over the bishops of mission lands came from missionary societies and religious orders, among which the French theologians were highly respected.

The ambiguity of Pope John's own vision was manifest in the sharp contrast between his choice of curial officers to head most of the preparatory commissions and the main conciliar commissions, and his opening speech at the first session of the council. The opening address complained about "prophets of doom" who find nothing good in the contemporary world and keep regretting the past glories of the Church, and it contained the unexpected confidence that such prophets of doom surround the pope. In the same address Pope John formulated his prospect for action in a theological axiom. The key to renovation lay, as he stated, in the distinction between "the substance of the faith" and "the way it has been expressed." Prophets of doom repeat old formulas that are no longer intelligible to the average person. They endanger the substance of faith because they confuse it with its old formulations. This distinction became a key to the debates of Vatican II.

Undoubtedly the distinction raises serious critical questions. In the Christology of Chalcedon one cannot separate the divine and the human in Jesus Christ, whose "two natures" are united "without confusion, change, division or separation." A similar unity unites the substance of faith and its formulation. The words are not the reality they designate. Words and their meaning, however, are one, for it is meaning that transforms sound into intelligible words. And meaning itself emerges, not just from sounds, but also rather from their recognized combination in keeping with a known grammar. Thus, two formulations of faith, say, in Latin and in Greek, designate the same reality, and correspond to one and the same substance of faith. Yet they also express diverse perceptions of this reality, that which is possible in Greek and that which is possible in Latin. Conversely, learning the faith in one language rather than another cannot be without influence on the way the reality is seen and understood.

Between the ultimate reality of God, or Christ, or the Spirit and its formulation, what Pope John called the substance of faith constitutes an intermediate level. It corresponds to the way words are understood and believers perceive the reality they signify. In Pope John's formula, this intermediate level was practically identified with the divine reality. But a rather different theology would follow if the substance were identified with the words. Then one would have to locate the level of orthodoxy: Is it in the formulation and its meaning, or in the reception and experience of the revealed wisdom? In the first case, strict formulations within each language of the world would be required for orthodoxy. In the second, wide differences in the formulations of faith would not necessarily impair the believers' orthodoxy. The Catholic mind has been more at home in the first perspective. Yet the second perspective, suggested in various ways in Protestantism and in Catholic Modernism, seems better to fit the structure of language[5].

In any case, Pope John could not enter into complex linguistic considerations; and there was a simple way to deal with his central concern. He could have avoided placing prophets of doom at key points in the preparation and the structure of Vatican II. The schemata that were proposed by the Preparatory Theological Commission, headed by Car-

5. I have developed this point in a French Book, *La Théologie parmi les sciences humaines*, Paris: Beauchesne, 1975.

dinal Ottaviani, were at odds with vital needs of the Church in sensitive areas of pastoral care and theological reflection. They maintained the ecclesiology of Bellarmine, the Counterreformation, and Pius XII. In making his appointments to the Preparatory Commissions, John XXIII behaved as he did when a few cardinals suggested a document on the perennial value of Latin as the language of civilization and of the Church. Issued in February 1962, the apostolic constitution, *Veterum sapientia*, was promptly forgotten. Given the main accents of modern culture, it was inapplicable.

In contrast with the curial structures of the Preparatory Commissions, the opening address of the council functioned as a scarcely veiled invitation to an open clash between the Roman curia and the bishops at large, between the *urbs* and the *orbis* of papal blessings. The decisive clash came when, on October 13, 1962, the majority refused to elect the conciliar commissions without having more time for consultation. Meanwhile, Pope John's innovative creation of the Secretariat for Christian Unity introduced a wedge of renovation in the conciliar structure along with ecumenical concerns and the willingness to listen to the voices of Orthodoxy and of the Reformation. This gave the *orbis* an edge over the *urbs*.

If indeed the immediate occasion for calling the council was provided by the post-war reconstruction and its accompanying turmoil, the remote cause was the repression of Modernism. The French Revolution and Darwinism had been at work, shaping politics and culture in the nineteenth century. But the Church's government still resisted modern culture. This made a Catholic renovation long overdue. There may have been something slightly Machiavellian in the mind of Pope John when he said that he was following an inspiration of the Holy Spirit, that the Church should look forward to a "new Pentecost," that the council should be more pastoral than dogmatic, and that it should fulminate no anathemas. The pope was shrewd enough to realize that a problem that is cultural and intellectual in regard to doctrine is political in relation to social institutions. The institution embodies the politics of its doctrine, while doctrine is the intellectual and spiritual justification of its politics. Therefore the Church should have the polity of its doctrine and the doctrine of its polity. The institutions of the Counterreformation no longer expressed the doctrine and the theology that were the most alive and promising. Conversely, the Church no longer had the polity of its theology. This was the datum from which Pope John started. The polity of Vatican I had attempted to substitute to the temporal authority of the popes a new sense of doctrinal authority. This was centered on the largely impractical doctrine of papal infallibility, impractical because its very nature makes the process too unwieldy for frequent use. Vatican II became necessary when the minority of 1870, which held the proclamation of infallibility to be inopportune, came to dominate the most creative movements in theological thought and Church renewal. The repression of Modernism brought about Vatican II because it deprived the Church of invaluable insights.

As far as John XXIII was concerned, the council would therefore close the period of the Counterreformation. It would silence the prophets of doom. Yet what would follow could hardly be a new Pentecost. Pope John had been a papal diplomat in Turkey and Bulgaria before being one in Paris, where he helped the transition from clerical collaboration with the Vichy régime to participation in the national reconstruction led by Charles de Gaulle. But Pope John was also, through his edition of the visitation reports of St. Charles Borromeo, a historian of the Tridentine reform. He knew that it takes decades, even centuries, before a general or ecumenical council becomes truly fruitful. I suspect, then, that he looked forward to a new form of catholicity, yet without discerning what this could be. A council would gain time to reach a consensus on this catholicity of the future, if not on Catholicism. The distinction between catholicity, one of the credal marks of the Church, and Catholicism, an institutional system of thought and government that had grown in the Middle Ages, had been clearly made by Pius XII in 1955.[6] Pius XII, however, did not realize that his own style of government carried to an extreme some of the least desirable features of Catholicism. Pope John perceived it. Yet he did not know how to reform the ultramontane Catholicism of the Counterreformation. The council was his way of gaining a reprieve for the Church.

It was the irony of history that the pope who started the council did not see the work through. Pope Paul VI (1963-1978) had a different vision. This vision inspired the hopes for the council that he expressed when, as archbishop of Milan, he answered Pope John's request, sent to all bishops, for suggestions and ideas for the council to come. After making some remarks on the preparation of the council, Montini listed four chief areas to be considered: doctrine, pastoral life, canon law, and

6. Address to the Tenth International Congress of Historical Sciences, 7 September 1955.

liturgy. The council ought to do more than update; it should reform. The doctrinal questions mentioned turned around relations between the natural order in its many dimensions and the supernatural, revealed order. Here one can detect Pope Paul's familiarity with the French theology of the time, and especially with the debate around Henri de Lubac's study of "the Supernatural"[7]. The future pope envisioned a series of dialectical relationships, between redemption and the natural good, Christian hope and human expectation, spiritual and political life, supernatural end and temporal action, worship and social obligation. Within the Church he looked at the relations between interior life and hierarchic institution, supernatural calling and the universal possibility of salvation, laity and hierarchy. The form of thought of the archbishop of Milan was manifestly dialectical.

Pope Paul's first encyclical, *Ecclesiam suam*, is divided in three sections: (1) the Church's awareness of being the Church; (2) the council as a high moment of this awareness; (3) the dialogical structure of the Church. This third section has received the closest attention, not least at an international congress on *Ecclesiam suam* (Rome, October 24-26, 1980). The encyclical discussed the nature and condition of true dialogue, the Church being in a continuous dialogue with the world and with all Christian believers. The Italian version, which is presumably the original text, refers to two aspects of this dialogue: *reformazione* (reform) and *renovazione* (renewal). The official Latin text, however, reduces these two terms to one only, *renovatio*. Presumably, *reformatio* or *reforma* were not the proper words in the translators' mind. Whether this was for reasons of Latinity or for fear of Protestantism is anybody's guess.

At the congress of 1980, I drew attention to the pioneering dimension of the first section of the encyclical. Other Christians also share the consciousness of being the Church, which is indeed at the center of Catholic ecclesiology. The Orthodox Church is aware of being the Church of the Fathers. When they meet for the worship of word and sacrament and in the fellowship of Christian love, Protestant congregations also are aware of being the Church. Pope Paul hit on a

---

7. *Surnaturel*, Paris: Le Cerf, 1946; later republished as two volumes: *Le Mystère du surnaturel*, Paris: Le Cerf, 1965; *Augustinisme et Théologie moderne*, 1969. Montini's letter is printed in Latin with Italian translation in *Istituto Paolo VI, Notiziario* n. 6, May 1983, p. 41-52.

nodal point of the ecumenical situation, in an insight that has not yet been fully exploited. Following it would lead, I surmise, very close to an ecclesiology of "provisional churches." If the key to recognizing the Church is no other than the experience of being the Church, then it follows that all institutional contexts of this experience, marked by the passing contingencies of history, can only be provisional. The better an ecclesial institution acknowledges its evanescent character and the provisionality of its structures, the closer its members are to recognizing the kingdom of God, which is already present in the permanent core of the experience of being the Church of Christ. I would not guarantee that these dimensions were fully present in Pope Paul's mind as he issued his first encyclical. But this is largely irrelevant. As the second pope of Vatican II foresaw and understood the council, his explanation of it became part of the conciliar process. The council was located at a crossing of multiple convergences: of the traditional Catholic mind and the modern secular mind, of the Catholic, the Orthodox, and the Protestant experiences of being the Church, of polity and theology, of the institutions of Christianity and the substance of the Christian faith. Dialogue was the form that the updating of the Church would take.

Looking for the achievements of Vatican Council II, one spontaneously lists decisions in the area of doctrine, concerning the collegiality and the sacramentality of the episcopate, the Church's intended openness to the modern world, the reform of liturgy with its most striking feature, the adoption of vernacular versions of the canon of the mass, the Catholic principles of ecumenism, the rejection of the notion that Jews are a deicide people. Some of these items are indeed striking. The center of the council, however, does not lie in any of these points, but in the fact that two visions of the Church clashed under the vault of St. Peter's basilica. Favored in the curial offices in the Vatican, there was an ecclesiology of the institution and its powers, of hierarchy and authority, of magisterium and ministry. Inherited from Cardinal Bellarmine and the Counterreformation, it owed more to the Reformation, against which it was developed, than to the previous Western tradition. While it had inspired Popes Pius IX, Pius X, and, most recently, Pius XII, it was entirely foreign to the Oriental traditions and Churches that were represented at Vatican II by their patriarchs and bishops. Coming mostly from outside of Rome, there also was an ecclesiology of the divine presence experienced through faith in Christ.

The location of the council was itself symbolic. Vatican Council I, with a little over 700 bishops, met in the gospel side of the transept in St. Peter's basilica, which ends up in a courtyard of the Vatican. Vatican Council II, with more than 2000 bishops, met in the central nave of the basilica, the gates of which open on St. Peter's square and the perspective of the *Via della Conciliazione*. At Vatican I the ecclesiology of the Counterreformation crested; and the thought of the minority was absent at the proclamation of papal infallibility. But the minority did not protest in vain, for a broader ecclesiology reemerged at Vatican II, when the two approaches met in the central nave. This time, however, John XXIII and Paul VI understood what Pius IX could not grasp. In a world exhausted by two world wars, the Catholic Church wished to set an example of peace and harmony. The two conciliar popes did not accept that the Church is inexorably bound to old ways. They knew that obsolescence must be recognized before it is remedied, and that the most conservative institutions in the world, the religious institutions, can find in their depths the capacity to trace the parameters and to outline the basic methods of their own renewal. Renovation, however, is not automatic. It takes no less vision, determination, courage, and patience to carry out the task of reform than to initiate it. The conciliar process did not end when the council was officially closed. Vatican II still needed to be received and implemented, and thus to pass into the ongoing Catholic tradition.

CHAPTER I

ECUMENICAL ITINERARY*

This chapter will be very personal testimony, but the chief point that I wish to make is not personal at all. I wish to emphasize a principle that relates to the nature and the method of ecumenical theology. This principle can be briefly indicated before I try to spell it out at length. It is at bottom very simple, though it has enormous consequences in practice: Ecumenical theology cannot be done in the abstract. Unlike systematic theology, which can be conceived when sitting at a desk and then put down on paper, ecumenical theology cannot be invented after reading suitable books and articles and drawing on adequate dictionaries. An ecumenical thesis does not emerge from the gathering of scholarly evidence, after taking time for reflection, and then figuring out arguments and conclusions concerning some aspects of the ecumenical problem. It can only be the fruit of dialogue between ecclesial traditions. By its very nature it is theology done in one tradition in dialogue with another. As such it must necessarily be done in the concrete. Dialogue, even between traditions, is a dialogue of persons. It is not in their documentary fossilization that traditions enter into dialogue with one another, but only as they are living in the hearts of believers. These believers can be popes, bishops, theologians—all of them having a stake in institutional stability, and therefore engaging in such a dialogue with some difficulty, always a degree of determined self-control, and at times with unformulated reservations—or simply members of the people of God with no special axe to grind.

❧

As the Catholic Church had to face it in the 1960's, the question of ecumenism was not a matter of mere theory. It arose from living experience, and precisely from the intermeshing of the concerns of the different Christian traditions that met in 1910 at the International Missionary

* With minor alterations this chapter reproduces the Dehon lecture, given at Sacred Heart School of Theology, Hales Corner, WI, 9 February 1994.

Conference of Edinburgh. Since that epoch-making gathering the ecumenical fabric that is being slowly woven has incorporated threads from
the Orthodox and later from the Catholic traditions into the originally
Anglican and Protestant woof of the movement. As perceived in the
Catholic Church at mid-century the ecumenical dimension was clearly
seen at Vatican II in the decree, *Unitatis redintegratio*: "By ecumenical
movement one understands activities and initiatives that are started and
are organized in order to promote the unity of Christians in keeping
with the Church's diverse necessities and opportunities" (n.4).

That such initiatives belong to the Church's normal life stands in line
with the affirmation of pope Paul VI in *Ecclesiam suam*, that dialogue
is inseparable from the existence and the self-awareness of the Church.
Ecclesial self-awareness exists only in dialogical form. The Church
is in dialogue with itself as it fosters a permanent internal dialogue
among its members. It also lives in a dialogical relation with the world
and the culture in which the faithful live and pray. Ecclesial dialogue
is more than a matter of experience and expediency that could change
with circumstances. It is at the heart of the Church and pertains to its
being as community, because the Savior, Lord of the Church, is also
the Creator of the universe and of humankind, and because the Word
who was conceived as man by the woman Mary is never estranged from
the divine Spirit who calls the creation to life and inspires the leaders
and prophets who will guide humanity to higher levels of culture and
spirituality.

The prescription of a dialogical mode of approach by Pope Paul and the
description of ecumenical tasks in the decree *Unitatis redintegratio* were
done, as it were, in advance, before the Secretariat for Christian Unity
initiated the bilateral dialogues with other Churches. They therefore
need to be tested by reference to the experiences that have taken place
since 1965.

One of the points that need testing emerges from Paul VI's division
of the ecclesial dialogue in two, internal and external. More exactly, one
should ask if theological dialogue with representatives of other Churches
is itself internal or external. In *Ecclesiam suam* Pope Paul offered the
image of concentric circles. The innermost circle represents the people
of God that is the Catholic Church. Next to it a slightly broader circle
extends to all the Christians who by faith and baptism are related to the
Catholic Church in a real though imperfect communion. There is a still
wider circle, which includes all those who believe in one God, whom

the Koran calls the People of the Book. At a further remove from the center is the circle of those who are religious without being monotheists in the strict sense. The great religions of Asia and the animism of allegedly primitive tribes might belong here. Next one finds the circle of agnostics who, without excluding God, are not committed to a positive religious belief. Then there is a circle of humanists who do not believe in God, yet who find a philosophical reason to be devoted to humanity, which then takes the place of God in the teleology, if not the etiology, of their life. Then also one could think of a circle of tolerant or indifferent atheists, and finally of militant atheists and anti-religious people.

In this perspective the ecumenical dialogue seems to be cast in an external mode. From within it extends out to reach those who stand outside the Church's inner circle. Whether or not this was truly the thought of Paul VI can hardly be ascertained. Yet it probably was, as it squared with sincere concern to affirm, with Vatican II, that a real though imperfect communion persists between Catholics and other Christians, at least by virtue of baptism and faith, often also by virtue of eagerness to hear the word, to receive divine grace, to celebrate God's mercy in thanksgiving, and to seek for Christian perfection. The institutional turn of mind, which had its classical formulation in the ecclesiology of Robert Bellarmine, remains to this day deeply embedded in the Roman mentality. In its eyes a dialogue of imperfect communion remains, so to say, ad extra insofar as it is distinguished from the dialogue of perfect communion that is believed to take place within the Catholic Church.

Here lies precisely, in my mind, the fundamental ecumenical question: When one takes part in the commissions that have been created all over the world to dialogue with Orthodox, Ancient Oriental Orthodox, Anglican, Lutheran, and Protestant Christians, are we only at the threshold of the Church, along with interested inquirers who stand, like Jewish proselytes, outside the gate? Are we in the margins? Or are we not indeed functioning within the circle of the People of God, which extends in some way to our partners in dialogue? Insofar as dialogue with Christians is ecclesial dialogue, it cannot be, I would think, outside the Church.

It may be difficult for many today to imagine such a remote time as the years before Vatican II. Needless to say, I am not among them. I was ordained in 1947, shortly after the end of the Second World War; and the period between the two wars remains very much alive for me since it was the theater of my formative years. In the part of France where we lived it was possible, on the radio, to hear Adolf Hitler make his speeches across the border. There were rumors of war, especially after the start of the civil war in Spain and when Mussolini engaged in an obsolete imperial conquest in Ethiopia. We were aware of the dangerous environment in which we lived.

This danger served in part to accentuate the tragedy of Christian divisions. I was aware of these chiefly because my mother always spoke of Protestants with great respect. Her paternal grandfather, whom she had known, had been born into the Reformed Church of Alsace and Lorraine. He remained a Protestant and worshipped in the Temple of my home city. Much later, when I did genealogical research on my father's side, I also discovered Lutheran ancestors, whom my father did not know about. I even saw the record of the reception in the Catholic Church of my direct ancestor, Elizabeth Domme, a German from the Palatinate, who, according to this document, renounced *haeresim lutheranam* on the feast of the Epiphany, January 6, 1776.

In addition to family ties and circumstances, I eventually entered a religious community with an ecumenical tradition. After spending two years in the diocesan seminary of Nancy, I joined the Augustinians of the Assumption (Assumptionists), whose founder, Emmanuel d'Alzon (1810-1880), had a keen interest in Orthodoxy. In keeping with the founder's will the Assumptionists still identify working for the unity of the Church as one of their basic purposes. In fact, when John XXIII announced the call of a council I was already well committed to the cause of ecumenical theology. For several years during my studies in Lyon the superior of the house was a well-known Byzantinist, Sévérien Salaville, who had spent many years in Athens. Another member of the community, himself a professor of Byzantine theology and an author with a considerable output, was Martin Jugie. Later I took part in unofficial theological conversations, in London with Anglicans, in Paris with members of the French Reformed Church, in New York City with Orthodox theologians. I cannot, however, pinpoint a moment when I began to think that I should work in relation with the ecumenical movement. It was clear in my mind, when I was given the opportunity to obtain a doctorate in theology, that I wanted to relate my work to the search for Christian unity. In fact the first topic that was suggested to me for a doctoral thesis was directly connected with French Protestantism, but I soon gave it up on advice from Henri de Lubac. Eventually, however, my thesis at the *Facultés catholiques de Lyon* was in the area of the theology of St. Bonaventure.

After finishing my doctoral studies I spent three years in England, where a newly formed English province needed instructors for a scholasticate that was projected. There, in Surrey, I lectured in apologetics or fundamental theology. I took occasion of these years to read Anglican authors, and I got to know personally several Anglican clergy, while I also discovered a variety of Catholicism that was entirely new to me, defensive, distrustful, and rather ignorant of anything that was not Roman Catholic, a Catholicism for which the central dogmas were the authority of bishops and papal infallibility, and which by the same token avoided whatever could be taken for an interest in ecumenism.

As a priest of my acquaintance formulated it: "The only thing I am willing to discuss with Anglicans is the principle of authority." During this time, nevertheless, I attended some unofficial meetings in London between a few Anglican and Catholic theologians. Things have changed considerably in Great Britain since those pre-conciliar days.

After three years in England I spent some fifteen months in Paris. There I composed my first book, a collection of prayers for Christian unity, which a publisher invited me to do. In 1954 I also published a French a volume that came out in English in 1955 under the title, *The Catholic Approach to Protestantism* (New York: Harper). This was a programmatic description of the requirements of an ecumenical understanding of Protestantism. I also, in 1959, published a major study of one of the basic problems of the Reformation, the problem of tradition and Scripture (*Holy Writ or Holy Church. The Crisis of the Protestant Reformation*, New York: Harper, 1958). The idea for this book had been conceived in Paris, where I also began the relevant research. The topic of Scripture and tradition has since then kept my attention through a number of publications. In Paris also I obtained a better knowledge of the Reformed Church of France, as I was soon invited to take part in a monthly gathering of Reformed and Catholic theologians. The future Cardinal Daniélou was one of them.

I came to New York City at the end of 1952, on the understanding that I would be free to work toward an ecumenical apostolate. In keeping with my theological training and interests, however, I conceived an ecumenical apostolate as more intellectual than pastoral, more theological than immediately practical. In fact I landed in New York with the names of two persons that I was told I ought to contact. Maurice Villain, S.M., a fervent ecumenist, who had recently traveled in the USA, recommended that I visit a Catholic lady of the Byzantine rite, Helen Iswolsky (1896-1975), and an Anglican lady, Barbara Simonds (d.1993).

Helen, then a professor of Russian at Fordham University, had founded "The Third Hour," a discussion group that brought together Russian Orthodox and Catholics for theological exchange, along with a smaller number of Episcopalians and Protestants. She invited me to the meetings, which I attended regularly until Helen retired from Fordham, and moved to Seton Hill College in western Pennsylvania. I got to know her well and to appreciate her ecumenical commitment. When, a few years later, Helen retired again from Seton Hill she moved to the Catholic Worker farm in New York State, for she had been a close friend of Dorothy Day for many years.

Helen was a woman of vision[1]. A former Russian Orthodox, she did not think she had left orthodoxy when she entered the Catholic Church. Rather, she had, somewhat like Soloviev, opened her heart to a more universal horizon than that of Russia. The daughter of the last ambassador of Czarist Russia to Paris, she had remained in France after the Soviet revolution. She was a profoundly religious person and a Benedictine Oblate of the Abbey of Regina Laudis. She had been familiar with philosophers, writers, and artists in Paris. She knew Nicholas Berdiaev and the expatriate American novelist Julian Green. In New York she was close to Alexander Kerensky, the prime minister who had been thrown out by Lenin in 1917. She frequently visited him and read to him when he became practically blind. In 1940, during the German invasion, she had fled Paris for southern France. In 1941 she had left France for the United States, as she was afraid that the German armies would invade the "free zone" in the South, as they in fact did after the landings in North Africa.

Barbara Simonds I met only once. She was chiefly known at the time for having organized some of the first ecumenical pilgrimages from the USA to the city of Rome by way of Canterbury. She was totally devoted to the project of reunion and very enthusiastic. Yet I found her theology

---

1. Helene Iswolsky, *Light Before Dusk. A Russian Catholic in France*, 1923-1941, New York: Longmans, Green & Co., 1942 (about the thirty years she lived in France); and *No Time to Grieve. An Autobiographical Journey*, Philadelphia: Winchell Company, 1985.

rather bizarre. The basis on which, as she explained it to me, reunion ought to take place struck me at the time, as not only untraditional, but also inapplicable. She thought that the pope should be considered the successor, not of Peter, but of Joseph, husband of Mary, adoptive parent, protector, and provider. This could have been a fruitful line to follow if there was some historical background for the principle. As adoptive parent, protector, and provider of the faithful, the bishop of Rome could cut a less triumphalist figure than has been the case. But the papacy developed long before there was any theological reflection on Joseph. When Joseph appeared in the Christian tradition it was not in theology but in spirituality, as a model. One of the first times his name appears in spiritual literature is, I believe, in the monastic rule of St. Fructuosus of Braga (seventh century). And it was much later still that the figure of Joseph gained popularity in piety, notably through the example of the great Teresa de Avila. This was much too late to recast the understanding of the primacy of the bishop of Rome and its exercise.

As I tried to find who, in New York City, had an interest in ecumenical relations and in the theology of ecumenism, I got a taste of what was then the standard American Catholic aloofness from ecumenism. The superior of the house where I lived, at the church of Our Lady of Guadalupe, had suggested that I talk with a diocesan priest who was known for his good relations with Protestants at Union Seminary and his general interest in ecumenism. This was the pastor of Corpus Christi church, Msgr John Ford. When I visited him, however, the main thing he said was: "If you are interested in ecumenism, take the next ship to Europe."

In fact there was much more in New York City than Father Ford admitted. There already was a meeting ground for Orthodox and Catholics who gathered regularly to talk about the theologies of the two churches, namely, the Russian Center at Fordham University. I actually paid a visit to the director. Fr Wilcox, S.J., however, had no special reason to be acquainted with my name, and he politely declined to invite me. A few weeks later he changed his mind, because the Russian Orthodox theologian, Alexander Schmemann, whom I had met at The Third Hour, insisted that I must join the group.

On the Catholic side there were the three or four Jesuits of the Russian Center, and also Gustave Weigel, who came from Woodstock College, two professors from St. John's Seminary in Boston, and a priest of the Melkite Church. On the Orthodox side there were several regular participants from St. Vladimir Seminary, which was still located in New York City. George Florovsky and Alexander Schmemann were among them. The conversations were informal but solid. Occasional visitors were brought into the circle. I specifically remember Christophe Dumont, O.P., who must have been on the way back from Evanston after the second meeting of the World Council of Churches. While in New York I made the acquaintance of Paul Tillich, thanks to a common German friend. I even sat informally in some sessions of his course on the Reformation. I made use of the libraries of Union Seminary and of General Episcopal Seminary. After four years in New York City, one in Worcester, MA, at Assumption College, and another again in New York, at the church of Our Lady of Esperanza, I got regular teaching assignments, first in Pennsylvania (Mount Mercy College in Pittsburgh, today Carlow University), then at Pennsylvania State University, and later at the Methodist Theological School in Ohio. I chaired the department of theology at Mount Mercy College when John XXIII called the council that became Vatican II. Much to my surprise he appointed me consultant of the Secretariat for Christian Unity, and later *peritus* of the council.

One particularity of Vatican II is that it was much better prepared than any one of the previous councils. In what came later to be called the ante-preparatory period the bishops sent letters and recommendations about the coming council. The preparatory period was a time when the march of the coming council had to be somehow imagined, so that the commissions that were foreseen would be fully ready for their task. Texts had to be written in anticipation of eventual decrees.

The secretariat for Christian unity did not at first plan for a decree on ecumenism. Rather, it conceived its task as principally trying to find ways to insert an ecumenical note in as many documents as possible. In this spirit it adopted a report on the liturgical reform—which I myself composed—in which it reviewed which reforms would be important for an ecumenical rapprochement. The report insisted especially on reemphasizing the preaching of the Word and on restoring communion under both species. The secretariat forwarded this report to the commission for the liturgy, which in fact was already working along the suggested lines. Both points were covered in the reform that took place, though the second—communion with the chalice—on a more hesitant and restricted mode than I would have liked.

Only when it became known that the Preparatory Theological Commission, led by Cardinal Ottaviani, was preparing a document on the deposit of faith, which would endorse the theory of "two sources of revelation," which had come to the fore in the Counterreformation, did the Secretariat for Unity start discussing the question of tradition. Likewise it was only when it was known that the proposed constitution on the church would include a chapter on unity and reunion that the Secretariat began to draft a decree on Catholic principles of ecumenism. While it may not have seemed so to those who followed these events from a distance, the preparation of the council and the council itself meant hard work. And the brunt of the work fell on the consultants during the preparatory period and on the *periti* during the council.

From the moment we began work on the decree on ecumenism I was much involved in the discussion and the writing of it. At various times I was also involved, though less intensely and less continuously, with the declaration on Judaism and other religions and with the declaration on religious liberty.

Under the leadership of the late John Oesterreicher, a professor at Seton Hall University, there were several meetings, in New Jersey, of an unofficial consulting group on the Church and the Jews. We prepared a first version of a possible decree. The text, however, went much further toward proposing an interpretation of the relevant passages of the epistle to the Romans than the bishops were generally prepared to go. The text that was eventually adopted spoke about all religions, a point that was not anticipated at the beginning. This was done chiefly for the sake of bishops in predominantly Muslim lands. Yet it allowed the later creation by Paul VI of the Secretariat for non-Christian religions and its subsequent work. Regarding Judaism, the final text simply faced the most urgent pastoral problems: anti-Semitism, the occasional but inaccurate accusation of deicide against Jews, and the cleaning up of Christian education from anti-Semitic implications. It did not attempt, as had been hoped at the start in the American group, to clarify the Church's view of the covenant of God with the heirs of the old Israel. This question was actually to be raised some years later when Christian theologians began to rethink the implications of the covenant in light of the restoration of Israel as a modern state. The various proposals that were then made had been anticipated and debated in the preparation of the council, but in the absence of a formula of agreement that could be accepted by the members of the Secretariat they had not passed into the texts that were submitted to the council.

In regard to religious liberty there were two questions. The main one was to sort out the principle of religious freedom. Some theologians saw freedom of conscience as a hypothesis that is necessary in a divided or pluralistic culture in which Catholics live next to non-Catholic Christians, and Christians next to non-Christians, while they maintained the thesis that every nation or state has a basic duty to recognize the true revelation and what it implies for the society. Religious liberty was at best a useful compromise with secular society. Others, the majority, regarded religious liberty as an absolute principle, but with no agreement as to the ground that supported the principle.

In the Secretariat for Christian Unity and in the council at large there was no division on the principle, but there was one on the justification of it. Many, chiefly Europeans, followed the bishop of Bruges, Joseph de Smedt, who based the liberty of religion on the notion of the common good of society. This came from the notion that the natural law implies the duty to seek the common good. It was also related to the personalist philosophy of Emmanuel Mounier, which had a wide audience among French theologians. John Courtnay Murray, S.J., however, saw the freedom of religion implied in the rights of the individual conscience in a democratic society where all persons are equal before the law. The bishop of Pittsburgh, John J. Wright, spoke in the council, in one of his few interventions, along the lines of the first argumentation. Yet the second point of view was chiefly, though not strictly, American. I also heard an Italian *peritus*, Pietro Pavan, argue that, in keeping with contemporary legal practice, the council could affirm a position without tying it to a theological or philosophical justification. The decree itself, after much discussion, was a compromise between these different emphases.

During the last three sessions of the council I served every afternoon on the press panel that had been set up by the American bishops to answer questions from English-speaking journalists about the events of the morning session. This was not directly ecumenical, though not all the journalists were Catholic and there were occasions when Paul Blanchard sat among the journalists and asked questions. He was a prominent figure in POAU (Protestants and Other Americans United for the Separation of Church and State), an organization that was not usually friendly to Catholics.

One cannot speak of an ecumenical experience today without saying a word about the World Council of Churches. My acquaintance with the official ecumenical movement came gradually. At some time in the years of my theological studies during and after the Second World War, Sévérien Salaville gave me documentation he had kept from the early days of Faith and Order after the First World War. My attention was also brought to the WCC that would soon be launched in Amsterdam in 1948 by a somewhat bizarre event. I believe it was in 1946 or 1947 that someone rang the bell at our house in Lyon where I was living. He was a priest of our Dutch province, who was himself active in Catholic/ Protestant relations in the Netherlands. He had heard in his country that there was to be an important ecumenical gathering in the city of St-Etienne in France. He had gone there by train with some difficulty, for trains were still few at that time. And he had discovered on arrival that what he had heard was a false rumor. So he came to our nearest house—in Lyon, – before returning to the Netherlands.

In 1954, when I was still in New York City I formed the project of going to Evanston to observe the general assembly of the World Council of Churches. I offered to write articles about it for a publication in Paris and for another in the Netherlands. I had already obtained from the WCC the official status of a journalist when the archbishop of Chicago, Cardinal Stritch, forbade all Catholics to attend the Evanston assembly. However, I did not think that this decision applied to someone who would simply report on the meeting. I was therefore one of the few Catholics who followed the Evanston assembly directly. I was also involved in the conference in another way. As he spent a few days in New York City on the way to Evanston, Dr. Visser't Hooft called me by phone and asked if I would put into English an essay that Yves Congar had written on the theme of the conference, Christ, the hope of the world. A translation had been planned under Congar's supervision, but if it was in print it had not yet reached Visser't Hooft. I made the translation, which was available to the delegates at Evanston, though Congar's English version was printed in the acts of the Conference.

❦

In 1963 I was among five official observers who were sent to the Faith and Order conference of Montreal by the Secretariat for Christian Unity. There I took part in the work of the commission that composed the often-quoted report, "Tradition, traditions and the process of tradition." The observers' chief task was, of course, to observe. Yet their remarks were welcome and the chair of this commission, the Norwegian Einar Molland, made no distinction among the participants and occasionally asked me for suggestions. The report in question made tradition one of the notable points of convergence between Catholic and Protestant theologies in the wake of Vatican II and the constitution *Dei Verbum* on divine revelation.

The chief originality of the ecumenical impetus that came from Vatican II was the initiation of a series of official bilateral dialogues between the Catholic Church and most other Christian traditions. This was naturally the task of the Secretariat for Christian Unity (renamed, Council by John Paul II in 1988), which has organized a number of international dialogues. I was named to the team of ARCIC-I that produced the now famous "Final Report" in 1981; and since 1983 I have been in dialogue with the World Methodist Council. But I wish to draw attention to the American dialogues, which deserve to be better known that they are. A number of national conferences of bishops, and especially the American conference, soon began similar ecumenical dialogues in their country or region. The American dialogue of Catholics with Lutherans was formed in the last year of the council, and likewise the dialogue with the Episcopal Church. I have been involved from the start in both of them. The achievement of the dialogue with Lutherans are well know, with its eight agreed statements, that go from "The Nicene Creed" (1965) to "The Apostolic Tradition" (1992), by way of statements on "One Baptism for the Forgiveness of Sins" (1966), "The Eucharist" (1967), "Eucharist and Ministry" (1970), "Papal Primacy and the Universal Church" (1974), "Teaching Authority and Infallibility in the Church" (1980), "Justification by faith" (1985), and "The One Mediator, the Saints, and Mary" (1991).

The work of ARC-USA is also well worth studying, although it has not been so well advertised or reviewed, is not of the same consistent excellence, and has been overshadowed by the Final Report of ARCIC-I. It has been generally focused on the nature of the Church and particularly on the Church as Communion. Let me mention its statements on "The Purpose of the Church"(1975), and on "Images of God. Reflections on Christian Anthropology" (1983), a topic that was raised by the ordination of women and that still needs serious attention. For a few years I also was in dialogue with the United Methodist Church, when it produced a statement on "Holiness and Spirituality of the Ordained Ministry" (1976).

Undoubtedly, the ecumenical movement has, from a Catholic point of view, encountered some unexpected drawbacks. One of these was precisely the unilateral decision of the Episcopal Church to ordain women, in spite of the known reluctance of Orthodoxy even to examine the question, and of the official opposition of the Catholic Church. The danger is not that dialogue will cease. It is that, in spite of the assurance of Vatican Council II that the Church stands in constant need of purification (UR, n.6), the positions will so harden as to become practically irreformable. The weakness of the theological arguments against the ordination of women should not blind us to the much more radical statement of pope John Paul II, that the Church does not consider itself "authorized" to ordain women. But, as everyone admits, the question is not answered in the Scriptures or in the early tradition of the Church, where it was not even raised. In keeping with the Catholic understanding of tradition, one cannot expect new revelations about such a matter. One may then ask: Who can authorize the Church to do what has never been done, if not the Church itself as it is guided by the Holy Spirit to act upon new discernments of the signs of the times?

Obstacles, however, should not be seen as merely negative. In divine providence they must have a positive side. They should be regarded as challenges rather than denials, the opening of new perspectives rather than as a closing of ways. To give an example, pope Paul wrote that the ordination of women in the Anglican Communion was "a new and grave obstacle" on the path to unity. He rightly assessed the gravity of the matter, although the newness was not so striking, since women have been ordained in a number of Protestant churches since the middle of the nineteenth century. At any rate, the present divergence in sacramental policy between Roman Catholics or Orthodox and Anglicans should be seen as an invitation to review the broader question of Christian anthropology, and to do this together as a contribution to the ecumenical theology of tomorrow. Ordination does not only raise a question of sacramental theology and practice. It goes to the heart of a much more central problem: Since it is in any case a human person who is ordained to a special participation in the priesthood of Christ, it is of major importance to determine what elements are constitutive of the human person. When theology thought and spoke in terms of matter and form, it could logically locate sexuality in matter, which, in the Aristotelianism of St. Thomas, is the source of individuation, and therefore is not indifferent to what is constitutive of the human person. But if theology no longer follows such categories, and sees the human person as a totality which is the image of God in nature and can be the likeness (similitude) of God in grace, then an entirely different Christian anthropology is open, which is bound to have consequences on the conditions in which a person can act liturgically in persona Christi. It seems to me that a broad consensus can be obtained on this question. Undoubtedly, the decision to ordain women should have followed rather than preceded such an investigation. But it is too late to change the fact, and regrets are not truly constructive.

It is on purpose that I have chosen this example of a type of research that needs to be done in common. I am convinced that the Christian theology of the twenty-first century will have to be done ecumenically or not at all. That is, each community in the spectrum of Christian churches, each strand among the Christian traditions, will have to recognize the others as its own and will have to draw from their tradition and experience, for this belongs to the nature of catholicity. The communities that fail to do so it will slowly die from inbreeding. A tradition that is living finds strength and depth not only from the past that it carries but also from the future that it anticipates in hope. A tradition that no longer learns dies. The same point applies to a church. In order to be relevant to constantly changing and moving circumstances the Church has to learn from the culture. The truth that such a Church teaches has been learned from all those who by faith have witnessed to Christ, and who have sought and received a degree of understanding, which they have in turn passed on.

Regarding the individual believers whose joint testimony constitutes the Church's tradition one should make a last point: It is not the ecumenical itinerary of any one particular person that is important; it is the convergence of itineraries.

CHAPTER 2

THE DECREE ON ECUMENISM*

Pope John's perspective went much further than problems of power and authority. While Pius XII had favored a modem approach to Scripture, his theology had remained squarely within the parameters of the Counterreformation. Nothing less than the nature of theological thought was now at stake: Should the theology of the schools be a mirror of the thought of the current pope? Is the primary task of theologians to provide a theological justification for the acts of the hierarchy? Or, if "the bishop is the official teacher in the Church"—as the bishop of Nottingham put it in his introduction when, in the fall of 1968, I gave the Firth Lectures at the University of Nottingham—is it really the theologian's function to explain the bishop's teachings?

John XXIII had enough experience of the Orthodox Church and its ethos to realize that Pius XII and his predecessors had unwittingly led the Catholic Church into a blind alley. Calling a council was his way to get the entire Church involved in a critical self-examination that was long overdue. From his studies on St. Charles Borromeo he knew that in the Catholic tradition the bishop is not only the chief officer of the diocese he governs, but is also the representative of all the baptized in the diocese. If only bishops in principle attend the council with a right to vote, they do this in the name and for the sake of their diocese, in communion with the lay people, the deacons, and the priests. Furthermore, at Vatican II, as also at Vatican I and at Trent, most of the work behind the scenes was done by conciliar *periti* appointed by the pope. Without the theologians the bishops would have had no texts to discuss.

* In substance this chapter reproduces a lecture given at Boston College on 11 November 2002 under the title, "*Unitatis redintegratio* and the updating of the Church;" in a slightly different form entitled, "The Decree on Ecumenism. Forty-years later," it was also given in Ottawa before the Life and Witness Commission of the Canadian Council of Churches on 4 October 2004; it is printed in this form in *Ecumenism*, n.157/158, March/June 2005, p.5-19 (Canadian Center for Ecumenism, Montreal).

ё

When, from 1960 to 1962, the newly created Pontifical Secretariat for the Unity of Christians met as a preparatory commission of the council, there was at first no thought of composing a decree on ecumenism. The task of the Secretariat, as the first secretary, Jan Willebrands, explained it to me when I arrived for the first meeting, was to make sure that whatever the council would decide had an ecumenical dimension. It was understood that the Theological Commission, headed by Cardinal Ottaviani, was preparing a decree on the Church, in order to complete the task that was unfinished when Vatican I ended abruptly on July 18, 1870, when the bishops of France and of Germany hurried home, as war between France and Prussia was believed to be imminent. (The war was in fact declared on July 19). There had been some interest, under Pius XII, in calling all the bishops together to bring Vatican I to an official end. John XXIII, however, did not wish to prolong Vatican I. He wanted a new council, with a new agenda. How the Theological Commission conceived its task, however, was largely unknown outside of it, although one suspected that it would work in keeping with the thought of its president, Cardinal Ottaviani.

The Secretariat for Unity had to steer between two points. The first was the formal intention of John XXIII to widen the ecumenical opening. The second was a widespread ignorance of the ecumenical movement among the voting members of the council. Inadvertently the pope's decision to invite Orthodox and Protestant observers gave rise in some quarters to the assumption that the role of the Secretariat would be limited to taking care of these visitors. The membership of the Secretariat, however, clearly indicated that it would be more than a welcoming committee. While Cardinal Bea's scholarship gave him a good knowledge of Protestant exegesis and exegetes, the secretary Willebrands had extensive ecumenical experience, in the Netherlands particularly, and in Europe generally.

The members of the Secretariat, chiefly bishops, were selected from areas where Catholics were neighbor to Orthodox, Anglicans, or Protestants. A few priests were also members: Charles Boyer, SJ, James Cunningham, Paulist, Canon Gustave Thils, Msgr Michele Maccarone. The consultants were chosen from several sources: the unofficial Catholic Conference for Ecumenical Questions, created on Willebrands' initiative in 1952, the *Groupe des Dombes* in France, the Jäger-Stählin circle in Northern Germany (Joseph Hofer, Hermann Volk), religious communities with a traditional interest in unionism or ecumenism (the Benedictine monastery of Chevetogne, the Society of the Atonement, the Augustinians of the Assumption), and theologians who were already involved in ecumenical relations (Pierre Michalon, S.S., Christophe Dumont, O.P., Gustave Weigel, S.J., and also, because of their knowledge of Judaism, John Oesterreicher, Gregory Baum, OSA, and Abbot Leo Rudloff, OSB). In practice Cardinal Bea made no distinction, in meetings and activities, between members and consultants.

I need not go into details concerning the work of the Secretariat for the Unity of Christians in its task as a preparatory commission of the council[1]. In a word, the Secretariat tried several approaches, with discussions and eventually drafts on the Word of God, on the Week of Prayer for Christian Unity, on the nature of the ecumenical movement (called, the "central ecumenical question"), on freedom of conscience, on the meaning of Judaism for Christians, in the hope that one or more of these drafts would serve the needs of the council. From the beginning the Secretariat also looked ahead to the post-conciliar period, when concrete ecumenical initiatives would need to be guided by some sort of an official directory. Its extended reflection on the central ecumenical question was in large part an anticipation of what would follow the council.

As the first session opened in 1962 the Secretariat was ready to act in order to stress the ecumenical dimension of the council, and to react to what other conciliar commissions would propose. The commentaries and histories that have been published since the council have generally missed the unique place of the Secretariat. It was the only one among the preparatory commissions that was, by the nature of its mandate, entirely turned to the future. Since most of what could be called precedents were negative, it had no tradition to guide it. This left it at the same time free of impediments, and dangerously open to questioning and criticism on the part of curial officials who followed a long-tested *stylus curiae*. What theology it could argue from was impressive but recent. The works of Yves Congar (1904-1995), Henri de Lubac (1896-1991), and Jean Daniélou (1905-1974) in France, those of Karl Adam (1876-1966), Karl Rahner (1904-1984), and the activities of *Una sancta* in Germany, the writings of Otto Karrer (1888-1976) in Switzerland, the early insights of Vincent Pallotti (1795-1850) in Italy, could serve

---

1. The lectures were published in a French translation: *La Religion à l'épreuve des idées modernes*, Paris: Le Centurion, 1970.

it well. None of these sources of ecumenical thought, however, had been endorsed by the curial offices, which on the contrary felt a natural affinity with the militant theology of the Counterreformation.

The other conciliar commissions dealt, either with traditional topics (the nature of the Church, the role of the hierarchy, the updating of liturgy, the proper status of the Eastern Churches, the formation of seminarians), or with specific problems of modernity (relating to education, the place and tasks of the laity, religious communities today, the media of social communication). In all these areas there were relevant precedents in past discussions of similar questions and in papal writings and speeches. In contrast, most precedents being negative, the task of the Secretariat was new. The only way it could proceed was to take a fresh look at the present, in order to shape the future unencumbered by the negative positions of the past. There ensued, among members and consultants, a progressive outlook, resolutely optimistic, in regard to the questions to raise, the perspectives to open, the methods to use. The work was clearly focused on development, without any attempt, however, to refine the theory and take sides among the various proposals dealing with the elusive concept that John Henry Newman's *Essay on the Development of Christian Doctrine*, in 1845, had drawn to the forefront of theological concerns.

If no theology of development has prevailed among the many that have been suggested since 1845, there nevertheless has been sufficient theological and historical reflection to say that, if the Church has indeed developed in its shape, and its doctrine has developed in its formulation, these developments are essentially related to the dimension of hope that is inherent in the credal mark of the Church, catholicity. The Church is confessed to be one, holy, catholic, apostolic. Catholicity, however, is not identical with geographic universality. It has a thickness that is measured by its capacity to embrace the future. Apostolicity draws its standard from the past of the Apostles and their teaching, which had its direct origin in the words and acts of Jesus. Catholicity looks for norms in the eschatological future when God will be all in all. In breadth it is potentially coextensive with the universe and the infinite greatness of God's design for all creation. In depth it is correlative with the active presence of divine grace at the most profound level of creaturely being, in the infinitely small and the infinitely great. In both perspectives catholicity is the realm of theological hope.

In all its work the Secretariat for Unity was inspired by this hope. It strove to keep the horizon of catholicity in sight, and to trace a path in the perspective of an open future. This, I believe, explains much in the methodology of the Secretariat during the council itself, as one may see in the first major problem it encountered. If it was natural for the Theological Commission, with its close ties to the Holy Office, to attempt to control all doctrinal formulae used by the conciliar commissions, it was equally natural for the Secretariat to assess the potential impact of statements in light of the ecumenical situation, and their relevance to what should be the Catholic Church's ecumenical commitment.

There were thus at the council two commissions with a potentially universal responsibility. The one, guided by Cardinal Ottaviani, saw it as its duty to bring the recent past to inform the present as totally as possible. The other, under Cardinal Bea, saw its task as foreseeing and preparing the future on the basis of a more biblical and patristic past. In the mind of John XXIII these were not contradictory orientations, as one could see in his decision, when the majority of bishops rejected the draft of the Theological Commission *De fontibus revelationis* ("On The Sources of Revelation"), to create a mixed commission, half of its members being selected by Ottaviani from the Theological Commission, the other half by Bea from the Secretariat for Christian Unity.

The Theological Commission made it urgent for the Secretariat for Christian Unity to draft a decree on ecumenism when it included a chapter *De oecumenismo* in its schema *De ecclesia*. This chapter was a total disaster. It renewed the invitations of Leo XIII and Pius XI to other Christians to come back to the fold under the authority of the Vicar of Christ on earth. Meanwhile, the Commission for the Oriental Church was also preparing a draft on the unity of the Church. Entitled, *De Ecclesiae unitate* 'Ut omnes unum sint,' this text acknowledged the Orthodox Churches as true Churches in apostolic succession. It presented the unity of Christians as a reunion through restoration of communion with the bishop of Rome. Given these contradictory orientations and the general dissatisfaction with the Theological Commission's proposal on the Church, Pope John told the Secretariat for Unity to prepare a decree that would take account of the diverse concerns of the Theological Commission and of the Commission for the Oriental Churches.

While Bea was doing appropriate diplomatic gestures toward some of the reluctant cardinals, the theologians of the Secretariat worked on a broad outline: (1) General principles; (2) Application to Orthodox/Catholic relations; (3) Application to Protestant/Catholic relations. Questions relating to Old Catholics, who are not quite Orthodox, and to Anglicans, who are not quite Protestant, would find their place during the redaction of the text.

Several passages in the decree, as it was adopted, on November 21 1964, by 1960 votes against 164, need special attention. These concern, (1) the nature and importance of ecumenical dialogues, (2) the principle of equality (*par cum pari*) in dialogue, (3) the ecclesial status of the Christian communities that are not in communion with the bishop of Rome, (4) the reference to the Anglican Communion, (5) the possibility of prayer in common (*communicatio in sacris*), and (6) the reference to sins against unity.

Pope Paul VI issued his first encyclical, *Ecclesiam suam*, on August 6, 1964[2]. This publication caused some concern, for when a general council is in session, the council is the supreme teacher, not the pope by himself. While no session was actually sitting in August, the third session was in preparation. It would have been appropriate to wait a little so that the encyclical could be issued together by the bishops in council. When one turns to the content and purpose of *Ecclesiam suam*, however, the reason for its publication appears. In part I, Paul VI answers a question that had been formulated by Cardinal Suenens in the great hall of the council: "Church of God, what do you say of yourself?" The pope analyses the self-awareness of the Church. In part II, he describes the most important quality of the Church's self-awareness, namely the dialogical structure of its life. It is probably not by accident that Paul VI signed the text on the feast of the Transfiguration of the Lord, a feast that Orthodox and Catholics celebrate on the same day. Precisely, the primary dialogue of the Church in patristic times was between its Greek and Latin halves, East and West, which ideally constitute the two lungs by which the whole Church breathes.

The timing and circumstances of the publication of *Ecclesiam suam* highlight its central message: The structures of the Church must be

2. This history is summarily described in Giuseppe Alberigo, *History of Vatican II*, vol. I, Maryknoll: Orbis, 1995, p. 263-271.

essentially dialogical. They must facilitate a constant dialogue of the Church, both with itself at all levels of its membership, and with the world, including other Christian communities and other religions. Ideally, in the Catholic Church nothing ever happens, Paul VI intended to say, that has not been prepared by dialogue. Given the sinful human situation, this ideal is seldom reached. Paul VI knew this as well any historian. It should nevertheless guide the council in better structuring the Church for dialogue. One may therefore assume from the encyclical that Paul VI felt impatient. The gathering of all the bishops was too slow and hesitant in placing dialogue at the center of its reforms.

The decree *Unitatis redintegratio* was promulgated on November 21, four months after the publication of *Ecclesiam suam*. It placed dialogue at the center. Since it was already in shape when the encyclical was composed, the second part of *Ecclesiam suam* constituted a powerful endorsement of what the projected decree was saying. Internal dialogue must be a reality in the Catholic Communion; and ecumenical dialogue, especially with Orthodoxy, should be at the center of Catholic concerns. Dialogue was in fact given pride of place in *Unitatis redintegratio* (n.9): We must get to know our separated brethren. Study is absolutely required for this, and it should be pursued in fidelity to truth in a spirit of good will. Catholics who already have a proper theological grounding need to acquire a more thorough understanding of all Christian traditions, their history, spiritual and liturgical life, doctrines, religious psychology, and cultural background. Most valuable for this purpose are joint meetings in which each side treats with the other with total parity, *par cum pari* (UR.n.9).

This is more than a description of what dialogues have been, more even than a prescription of what they ought to be. It implies a program for the whole Church. Catholics ought to know the soul of their estranged brothers. Estranged translates the Latin, *sejuncti*, not *separati*, for *sejunctio*, as Cardinal Antonio Bacci (1885-1971), a distinguished Latinist, reminded the bishops, is temporary, while *separatio* is permanent. The required studies to discover the truth should be made with an open heart. The truth in question covers the whole field of doctrine and history, spiritual life, culture, and religious psychology of the other Christians in dialogue with us. And the parties that meet in dialogue should be treated on an equal basis.

One can understand equality at the level of the individuals who take part in dialogue. Each participant must feel free to speak his or her mind.

Yet there is more to it. The participants should see their communities as themselves meeting *par cum pari* through their representatives. The equality in question must be ecclesial, in the sense that each Church is assumed to offer a valid way to God through Christ in the Holy Spirit. The members of the dialogue could not lead a discussion on an equal basis if each side in its heart held its own Church to be in some sense superior to, or truer, or more Christian, than the other. In practice this implies that each side regards the history, doctrine, and ethos of the other as somehow its own too. The peculiarities of both sides should be accepted and even owned by all. This requires much more than a program of occasional meetings. It is a proposal for a new solidarity among Churches that have been estranged for centuries, so that from now on each will strive to cherish the other and treat it as it hopes to be treated in turn.

In the document, known as the *Malta Report*, the Joint Preparatory Commission of the Catholic Church and the Anglican Communion, which met three times in 1967 and 1968, recommended that a first stage in dialogue consist in studying several "possible convergences of lines of thought" (n.6) between Anglican and Catholic theology, and that a "second stage of our growing together" be opened by "an official and explicit affirmation of mutual recognition by the highest authorities of each Communion" (n.7)[3]. In other words, dialogue should go beyond discussion and conversation. It should nurture a growing together of the Churches, based on sharing the same belief that the Church is founded on the revelation of God the Father, made known to us in the person and work of Jesus Christ, who is present through the Holy Spirit in the Scriptures and his Church, and is the only Mediator between God and man, the ultimate authority for all our doctrine. Each accepts the basic truths set forth in the ecumenical creeds and the common tradition of the ancient Church, although neither Communion is tied to a positive acceptance of all the beliefs and traditional practices of the other[4].

---

3. See "*Ecclesiam suam.*" *Première Lettre Encyclique de Paul VI.. Colloque International, Rome 24-26 octobre 1980*, Brescia: Istituto Paolo VI, 1982.

4. Alan C. Clark and Colin Davey, *Anglican/Roman Catholic Dialogue. The Work of the Preparatory Commission*, London: Oxford University Press, 1974; Joseph W. Witmer and J. Robert Wright, eds., *Called to Full Unity. Documents*

This recommendation is a good example of fidelity to the basic conciliar insight on the nature of ecumenical dialogue. The Churches that face each other in dialogue enter into a relation of sisterhood, the extent and the formal nature of which should be carefully discussed. On 9 July, 2000, I gave the keynote address at an *Orientale Lumen* Conference in Melbourne, Australia, on the topic of Sister-Churches[5]. I made the point that ecclesial sisterhood is the relationship that ties together the Ancient Oriental Church, the Orthodox Church, and the Catholic Church, in spite of their historical and theological differences. It implies what Carol Wojtyla, in 1969, called "intersubjectivity by participation[6]." I also suggested that those Churches that have inherited their sisterhood from their shared history before the divisions of the past should reflect on the extent to which they can acknowledge a sisterhood with the Churches of the Reformation. There exists an intersubjectivity by participation among all Churches engaged in dialogue, if at least the dialogue follows the lines that were drawn in the decree on ecumenism. The notion of intersubjectivity is itself very close to that of sisterhood. I said in Melbourne: "The Church must cultivate Sisterhood as a fundamental mark, a dimension, of its Catholicity[7]."

In this perspective one can rule out ecclesial sisterhood between the Catholic Church and the Churches that underwent the Reformation in the sixteenth century only if the ecumenical dialogue is brought to a premature end. Such a drastic measure, however, would considerably weaken catholicity. A catholicity that is closed upon itself and does not reach out to others in generous fraternity is less than catholic. Just as holiness must always be further purified (*ecclesia sancta simul et semper purificanda*, as said in *Lumen gentium*, n. 8), catholicity should be constantly self-enlarging. And this enlarging requires cultivating three qualities of ecclesial life, namely, unanimity of mind and heart, collegiality in action, subsidiarity in collaboration.

---

on Anglican-Roman Catholic Relations, 1066-1083, Washington: BCEIA, 1986, p. 3-14.

5. *Called to Full Unity*, 1985, p.9.

6. *Orientale lumen. Australasia-Oceania 2000. Proceedings*, Melbourne: Australian Catholic University, 2000, p. 1-22.

7. Karol Wojtyla, *The Acting Person*, Dordrecht: Reidel Publishing Company, 1979, p. 261.

I read my Melbourne paper just before the letter of 30 June 2000, on "the use of the phrase 'sister-Churches,'" that Cardinal Ratzinger addressed to the Presidents of the Conferences of Bishops, reached Australia. The letter accompanied a Note from the Congregation for the Doctrine of the Faith on "the expression 'Sister-Churches.'" The Note referred to fully flourishing sisterhood. However, following the way Paul VI, on October 26, 1970, envisioned the future embrace of the Anglican Communion as "ever-beloved sister" of the Catholic Church, sisterhood may also be seen as a partial relationship, that ought to be perfected until it can flourish fully[8]. It was in this spirit that in Melbourne I asked if the Catholic and the Orthodox Churches are prepared to think of the Protestant Churches, or some of them, in the perspective of ecclesial sisterhood, and if they are willing "to abandon some of their cherished points of view or practices in order to promote a closer sisterhood[9]."

The situation at the beginning of the twenty-first century shows that we have failed, even at the highest level, to exploit the insights of the Secretariat for Unity that were endorsed by the council. While the encyclical of John Paul II, *Ut unum sint* (25 May 1995), is unimpeachable in its appropriation of the principles of *Unitatis redintegratio,* the council's orientations have not been fully shared in some major offices of the Roman curia, as one can gather from the letter, *Dominus Jesus* (6 August, 2000). I do not myself take a dramatic view of this document. A "declaration" is the lowest in authority among the documents issued by the Holy See. And in any case, most of its contents refer to the question of the salvific dimension of non-Christian religions, not to dialogues between Churches.

What the letter suggests about Churches and ecclesial communities should be understood in light of the decree *Unitatis redintegratio.* There is no mystery about what the decree intended in using the expression, ecclesial communities. Three sorts of Christian communities were represented at the council by official observers: Orthodox Churches, Churches, Anglican or Protestant, that underwent the Reformation, and Christian Communities, issued from the Reformation, that do not

---

8. *Orientale lumen,* p. 12.

9. Robert Hale, *Canterbury and Rome, Sister-Churches. A Roman Catholic Monk reflects upon reunion in diversity,* New York: Paulist Press, 1982.

call themselves Churches. The formula, "Churches and Ecclesial Communities of the West", simply intended to imply that even these have an ecclesial dimension, because their members are Christian believers, and Christian believers cannot be unrelated to the Church of Christ.

There was in the expression no intention to decide what is or is not a Church. This was clearly stated by the archbishop of Westminster, John Carmel Heenan, on 7 October 1963, when he introduced the relevant section of chapter 3 of the decree in its final form[10]. In the absence of indications to the contrary one must hold that the text was endorsed by the bishops in the sense that was explained to them. There is no way to give the text another meaning. The assumption, which was not made in *Dominus Jesus*, but only in commentaries about it, that a Church presupposes a valid sacrament of orders, while an ecclesial community is only based on valid baptism, has no foundation in the intent of the Secretariat for Unity at Vatican II. It is a speculation that is without merit, and is demeaning to the sacrament of baptism. In fact, recent texts coming from the Holy See and from bishops use the expression, ecclesial community, in a loose sense, which can be applied to any Church, including the Catholic Church.

A word ought to be said about the specific mention of the Anglican Communion in n.13 of *Unitatis redintegratio*:

> …many communions, national or confessional, were separated from the Roman see. Among those in which Catholic traditions and institutions in part continue to subsist, the Anglican Communion occupies a special place[11].

The Secretariat did not specify what this place was[12]. At the same time it implied that other communions too have preserved some Catholic

---

10. *Orientale lumen*, p.20.

11. « *Loquentes in titulo de Ecclesiis et de Communitatibus ecclesiasticis, omnes comprehendere volumus qui nomine Christiani decorantur. Minime tamen in quaestionem disputatam intramus quaenam requirantur ut aliqua Communitas christiana theologice Ecclesia vocare possit* » (*Relatio super caput tertium*, in *Acta et documenta Concilii Vaticani II, Periodus III, part III*, vol. II, p.14).

12. « *Exinde a sede romana plures Communiones sive nationales sive confessionales sejunctae sunt. Inter eas, in quibus traditiones et structurae catholicae ex parte*

traditions and structures. Precisely, a longer description of the Anglican Communion could have caused surprise that nothing was said about Old Catholic or Lutheran Churches. The special place of Anglicanism was illustrated after the council by the international dialogue, ARCIC-I (Anglican Roman Catholic International Conversations). The *Final Report* of this commission, terminated in 1981 and published in 1983, embodied the successive reports of the dialogue: the *Windsor Statement* on Eucharistic doctrine (1971), the *Canterbury Statement* on ministry and ordination (1973), the *Venice Statement* on authority in the Church (1976), done under pope Paul, along with the second Statement on authority in the Church II (1981), that was finished under John Paul II. The *Final Report* was in fact put together in great haste. At the last meeting under Paul VI (28 August-6 September, 1979, in Venice) Cardinal Willebrands had reported that no deadline was in sight for this dialogue. Nevertheless, when the participants met again in Venice after the election of John Paul II (26 August-4 September 1980), they were informed that their next meeting would be the last (25 August-3 September 1981, at Windsor Castle).

It could have been expected that the publication of the *Final Report* would inaugurate the difficult process of the reception in the Catholic Church of documents drawn by officially appointed theologians of two Churches, working *par cum pari*. The process was all the more difficult as it was new. The last time something comparable had taken place was at the colloquy of Regensburg between Catholics and Lutherans in 1541. However, the agreement on Justification that was formulated in the *Regensburg Book* was rejected by Martin Luther and by Pope Paul III, although it was the joint work, among others, of Philip Melanchthon and Cardinal Gasparo Contarini. The team that composed it, at the Imperial Diet of that year, had been mandated by the emperor, not by the pope. In 1981, on the contrary, the commission had its mandate from Paul VI to examine the problems that have historically divided the sees of Rome and of Canterbury.

The critical reaction to *The Final Report* was issued in 1991, ten years after the end of the work. This excessively long delay illustrates a major problem. What has been conceived by one pope can be seen in a different light under his successor. One may presume that Paul VI had a process in mind regarding the reception of ecumenical statements. That

---

subsistere pergunt, locum specialem tenet Communio anglicana. » More detailed descriptions were proposed and discarded when the text was composed.

he had himself authorized their publication indicated at least that he considered them free of theological error, and that they did not open unacceptable perspectives. The decision to end this commission and create a new one, ARCIC-II, made of mostly new members, inadvertently introduced a glitch in the process of ecumenical relations that had begun with the Preparatory Commission in 1967 and its far-seeing *Malta Report* (1968). The problem of transition became evident when the members of ARCIC-I, some of whom were already on the way to Rome in the Summer of 1980, were informed by telegram that the joint commission had ceased to exist when Paul VI died, and that there could be no meeting until it was reconducted by the next bishop of Rome. ARCIC-I was duly revived by John Paul I, and then by John Paul II on the understanding that it would soon finish its work. For this reason *The Final Report* was hurriedly put together in 1981. ARCIC-II, when it was formed, adopted its own agenda[13].

Meanwhile, the reception of *The Final Report* had to be improvised. The text was submitted to the Conferences of Bishops, the reports of which, as it turned out, were not to be made public, but to be handed over to the Congregation for the Doctrine of the Faith, where most of the readers, however, had no accurate knowledge of Anglicanism. When it was finally released, the official response added nothing of substance to a critical evaluation that had been contained in 1982 in a letter from the Congregation for the Doctrine of the Faith to the co-chairs of ARCIC-I, before the National Conferences of bishops had time to examine the text with their local expertise, and to give freely their regional response. The reception was thus undermined from the start by overzealous officials!

What should one learn from this unfortunate episode? The canonical question of papal transition lies outside my purview. The theological lesson, however, is clear. As I explained it at the end of a book on Anglican ordinations[14], there can be no satisfactory answer to the question of their validity in Roman Catholic eyes as long as the critical stance of the Counterreformation is not balanced by a true desire for reunion. Only such a desire can give life to the new context that already exists,

---

13   See the joint reports, *Salvation and the Church* (1986), *Church as Communion* (1991), *Life in Christ: Morals, Communion, and the Church* (1994), *The Gift of Authority: Authority in the Church* (1999).

14.   *A Review of Anglican Orders. The Problem and the Solution*, Collegeville: Liturgical Press, 1990.

as was stated by cardinal Willebrands in a letter of 13 July, 1985 to the co-chairs of ARCIC, and was explained at length in a joint statement of ARC-USA[15]. Likewise, only a desire for reunion can overcome the more or less irrational fears that are fed, outside of the ecumenical commissions themselves, by the discovery of other theologies than those that have traditionally coexisted, more or less harmoniously, within the Catholic Communion.

Future relations between Catholics, both Roman and Byzantine, and Anglicans should be planned, as foreseen by the *Malta Report*, so that the two Communions may stop ignoring or criticizing each other, and rather go on to learn, theologically and practically, how to grow together. The tradition must look, not only back to the past, but also forward to the future. In this perspective, the beginning of the twenty-first century looks hopeful. The meeting of Anglican and Catholic bishops that took place at Mississauga, Ontario, in 14-20 May, 2000, inaugurated a new style of relationships, which is bound to open further horizons.

Precisely, the Malta report in 1968 recommended that bishops of the two Communions meet on a regular basis. The practice of holding local clergy meetings is already widespread, but such meetings should not be merely social. Care should be taken, especially at the top levels of leadership, that they not remain purely formal, but involve the Churches as such. Intermediary aims on the way to organic reunion would be joint pastoral care, the sharing of seminaries, the joint formation of clergy candidates, the joint teaching of catechism.

The *Malta Report* also recommended that the second stage of dialogue between the two Communions, the *Report* itself ending the first stage, "begin with an official and explicit affirmation of mutual recognition from the highest authorities of each Communion" (n.7). Precisely, at Mississauga the Commission endorsed "an Action Plan," which includes "the preparation of a Joint Declaration of Agreement." Thus the on-going dialogue of Catholics and Anglicans is catching up with the insights of the Preparatory Commission formulated shortly after Vatican II. Patience may some day be rewarded

Communicatio in sacris, "participation in sacred rites," was generally forbidden to Catholics by canon 1258 §1 in the Code of 1917: "It is not

15. *Anglican Orders: A Report on the Evolving Context of their Evaluation in the Roman Catholic Church*, Collegeville, MN: Liturgical Press, 1994.

licit for the faithful actively to assist, that is, to take part, in the sacred rituals of non-Catholics"[16] The second paragraph tolerated "a passive or merely material presence, for a civil or honorary purpose, with a serious reason that must be approved by the bishop in case of doubt, in funerals, nuptials or other solemnities, provided there be no danger of perversion or scandal." This canon implied an entirely negative view of Christian prayer outside of the Catholic Church. It made no distinction between Orthodox, Anglicans, Lutherans, and other Protestants, whose liturgical services seemed to be uniformly treated as heretical or pagan. The regulation, however, like the Code of 1917 in general, applied only to the members of the Latin Church, and there were areas where it remained a dead letter in relations between Eastern Catholics and Orthodox. Moreover, the canon was generally interpreted more strictly in English-speaking countries than on the European continent. In spite of relative leniency in some areas, the strict prohibition was not compatible with the ecumenical opening of John XXIII and what he desired Vatican II to do.

On its part, chapter XI of the *De Ecclesia* proposed by the Theological Commission expressed a degree of understanding of the contemporary ecumenical movement. It nevertheless maintained the unionist perspective of Leo XIII when it declared that the Catholic Church "lovingly invites the separated Christians to come to itself[16]." These ought "to return to unity,... which consists in unity of faith, of the communion of sacraments and of government,... in the unity of faith, of government and of communion under the one vicar of Christ." When it faced the question of prayer in common, the draft disparagingly called the Protestant Eucharist "a putative sacrament"; it alluded to "false liturgical prayers or even incorrect preaching," as if the preaching of Catholic priests was never incorrect! And it offered a long justification of the absolute prohibition of prayer in common.

I need not repeat what I have already written on the genesis of the passage of *Unitatis redintegratio* regarding *participatio in sacris*, prayer in common[17]. The text recommends common prayer for unity. It explains that prayer in common has a double purpose: to express the unity of

16. "*Haud licitum est fidelibus quovis modo active assistere seu partem habere in sacris acatholicorum*".

17. "*...amanter ad se invitat*" (Acta synodalia..., Periodus I, Pars IV, p.82, n.50); following citations: "*ad unitatem redeant,... in unitate fidei, communionis sacramentorum ac regiminis,... in unitate fidei, regiminis, et communionis sub*

the Church, and to bring about participation in the means of grace. As expressing the unity of the Church it does not generally belong where there is formal division. As participation in grace it is occasionally advisable. Since there is a discrepancy between these two aspects, the actual practice should be supervised by the bishop in light of all circumstances of place, time, and people.

When the text of Vatican II on prayer in common was composed, the national conferences of bishops were generally expected to have legislative authority, which still eludes them. Since circumstances vary considerably from one continent to another, and to a lesser degree from one country to the next, the decree assumed that norms for prayer in common need not be universal and may differ from one Episcopal Conference to another. This is why the council gave authority to the ordinary to approve *communicatio in sacris*, unless more universal norms have been determined. What is improperly called "intercommunion" can therefore be authorized in concrete cases by the ordinary. The sharing of Eucharistic communion in an inter-Church marriage or in an ecumenical dialogue would be in the spirit of the decree on ecumenism. This is evidently one of the ways in which two Churches can learn to grow together. The bishops who have used this provision, however, are far from numerous.

Future historians will note that a strange phenomenon took place at the beginning of the third millennium. The year 2000 had been prepared with enthusiasm and, at least in Rome, with considerable thought. *Tertio millennio adveniente* (10 November, 1994) outlined a Trinitarian program of preparation: God the Son, God the Holy Spirit, and God the Father would be celebrated successively in 1997, 1998, 1999, and the year 2000 would celebrate the entire Trinity together. In a surprising analogy John Paul II declared: "The year 2000 is the hermeneutical key to my pontificate." In 2000 the Jubilee was inaugurated ecumenically in a hitherto unheard of manner, when the archbishop of Canterbury and a representative of the Ecumenical Patriach opened the Holy Door of St. Peter's basilica together with the bishop of Rome. In 2001 the apostolic letter *Novo millennio ineunte* (6 January) celebrated the new

---

uno vicario Christi" (p.83, n.52); "*sacramentum putativum*" (p.85, n.54); "*preces liturgicae falsae vel etiam praedicatio non rect*"a (p.86, n.54).

millennium with an admirable optimism that was focused on contemplation of the face of Christ.

Nothing in these celebrations prepared the ground for what followed: a series of apologies for shortcomings and sins, the likes of which had never been heard in the entire history of the Church. A few examples will be sufficient. The document, *We remember. A Reflection on the Shoah*, published by the Commission for Relations with the Jews (16 March, 1998), duly noted: "The balance of these relations between Catholics and Jews over two thousand years has been quite negative". As he welcomed this document, John Paul II declared, "...the Church is aware that the joy of a Jubilee is above all the joy that is based on forgiveness of sins and reconciliation with God and neighbor." He then invited the faithful to examine their conscience: "She calls them to place themselves humbly before the Lord and examine themselves on the responsibility which they too have for the evils of our time." When it is put in those terms, the question of responsibility can only get a negative answer from most of the faithful, who bear no direct responsibility for the collective evils of their time.

In a homily for the conclusion of the Week of Prayer for Christian unity in 2001, John Paul II approached the question of responsibility from another angle. Looking forward to the new millennium he said:

> A fundamental task in this perspective is the purification of memory. In the second millennium we were hostile and divided; we condemned and fought one another. We must forget the shadows and the wounds of the past and strain forward to the coming hour of God (cf. Phil. 3:13). To purify our memories also means developing a spirituality of communion (*koinonia*) on the model of the Trinity, a communion which embodies and reveals the very essence of the Church.

Purification of memory, in this context, means forgetting the negative aspects of the past in order to launch forward into the future. This theme recurred in many later speeches and writings of Pope John Paul, notably in the encyclical *Novo millennio ineunte* (6 January 2001). The purification of memory was one of the major topics in St. John of the Cross's *Ascent of Mount Carmel*. It is effected, as the Mystical Doctor explained, through the theological virtue of hope, which always and in all things looks forward to the coming gifts of the grace of God. The Sanjuanist doctrine—with which John Paul II was familiar, since he wrote a doctoral thesis on the doctrine of faith according to John of the Cross—was designed for Christians who are called by divine grace to the mystical life.

The purification of a collectivity like the Church[18] can be conceived by analogy with the sacrament of reconciliation. Forgiveness requires repentance and, at least in the worst cases, demands a confession of sins. The absolution received may then initiate a healthy oblivion of the past. Similarly, the on-going purification of the Church may well inspire repentance and confession, so that oblivion, as in the case of the excommunications between Rome and Constantinople, may be arrived at by mutual agreement. In fact a number of events in recent years have reminded Catholics of errors in their past. Recurring questions relating to Pius XII and Jews, to the beatification of Pius IX and his role in the Mortara affair, to the wisdom of establishing a Carmel at the edge of the Auschwitz extermination camp, to the tolerance of pogroms, especially during the Crusades, have fed the urge to ask for vicarious forgiveness, be it long after the actors and collaborators of crimes against humanity have vanished from the scene.

The pope who initiated begging for forgiveness on behalf of the Church was Paul VI as he opened the second session of Vatican II on October 11, 1963. Addressing "the representatives of the Christian denominations separated from the Catholic Church," the pope said: If we are in any way to blame for that separation, we humbly beg God's forgiveness. And we ask pardon too of our brethren who feel themselves to have been injured by us. For our part, we willingly forget the grief endured during the long series of dissensions and separations[19].

The apology was conditional. It raised the possibility, but did not voice the conviction, that "we or our predecessors" deserve to be blamed for the separations. The decree on ecumenism went further, with an unconditional formulation: "The testimony of St. John is valid also in regard to faults against unity: 'If we say that we have not sinned we make him a liar and his word is not in us' (1 John 1,10). We therefore humbly ask God and our estranged brothers for forgiveness, as we also forgive our debtors" (n.7).

---

18. "Praying together. *Communicatio in sacris* in the Decree on Ecumenism," in Alberic Stacpoole, ed., *Vatican II Revisited*, Minneapolis: Winston Press, 1986, p.202-219.

19. "*ecclesia sancta simul et semper purificanda*" (LG. n.8).

These lines were composed by myself, when Willebrands asked me to propose a short text on sins against unity, while others—chiefly Pierre Michalon—wrote on the interior conversion without which there is no true ecumenism. Confessing sins and asking for forgiveness in the name of our ancestors in the faith express our desire for friendship with those who are still hurt by the fault, of our ancestors. It so happened that the text of UR. 7 bore fruit even before it was endorsed by the council. On January 6, 1964, less than two months after the debate on *Unitatis redintegratio* Pope Paul VI and Patriarch Athenagoras had their historic meeting in Jerusalem, which was itself opened the way to the joint declaration of December 7, 1965, when the pope and the patriarch declared the excommunications of 1054 "consigned to oblivion," in what they called a "reciprocal act of justice and forgiveness."

The decree on ecumenism was presented to the assembled bishops during the second session, on November 18. It was debated from November 21 to 27, and officially approved at the third session, the first vote on chapter I taking place on October 1, 1964 (1926, *placet*, 30 *non placet*, 209 *placet juxta modum*). When they presented and endorsed the decree, however, neither the Secretariat for the Unity of Christians nor the conciliar fathers intended to induce a collective examination of conscience on the whole range of past derelictions of duty by members and leaders of the Church. John Paul II gave the true sense of the text when he spoke of the purification of memory. The mutual gesture of committing past hurts to oblivion was an exercise in such a purification.

There is therefore a certain irony in that the formula of *Unitatis redintegratio* in regard to sins against unity served as a precedent for the numerous official apologies that have been made by bishops since the start of the third millennium. On March 12, 2000, John Paul II said in a homily:

> Let us ask pardon for the divisions which have occurred among Christians, for the violence some have used in the service of the truth and for the distrustful and hostile attitudes sometimes taken toward the followers of other religions. Let us confess even more *our responsibilities as Christians for the evils of today.* We must ask ourselves what our responsibilities are regarding atheism, religious

indifference, secularism, ethical relativism, the violations of the right
to life, disregard for the poor in many countries[20].

The pedophile crisis in the American Church has in turn multiplied
demands for apologies. Excessive apologies, however, may be rhetorical
devices rather than expressions of real sorrow, and thus could throw
doubt on the sanity of the whole process.

All this turmoil illustrates the fact that no ecumenical council has ever
been received without upsetting many of the faithful, including some of
the participants in the council. Heated controversies followed the Councils of Nicaea and Chalcedon. Implementation of the reform decrees of
the Council of Trent was slow. Vatican I started heavy debates on the
exact scope of papal infallibility, provoked the Old Catholic schism, and
led to the repression of Modernism. Vatican II is no exception. As the
decree on ecumenism declared, "there is no true ecumenism without
interior conversion" (UR. n.7). Interior conversion, the fruit of divine
grace, may require passing through the active and passive nights of faith
that are necessary to the purification of memory and of charity.

---

20. *Council Speeches of Vatican II*, 1964, p.146.

CHAPTER 3

FOR A THEOLOGY OF DIALOGUE*

In 1960 Canon Gustave Thils raised the question of the possibility of an ecumenical theology. He answered it affirmatively. An ecumenical theology, he wrote, can be either an "existential confrontation" between diverse traditions, or a "dimension" of all theology, bringing the experience of other churches to bear on the theology-making process of one church, or also a "particular discipline" functioning as a subdivision of systematic theology.[1] These three movements have now taken place. There are universities and seminaries that offer courses in these three areas: on ecumenics (third sense in Thils's nomenclature), on bilateral dialogues (first sense), on the perspective of ecumenical openings in the systematic elaboration of doctrine (second sense). The question may now be put in other terms than in 1960, however useful those terms were at the time.

No one in the developing ecumenical movement can help standing in the wake of the initiators of the movement, who legated to them two conceptions of ecumenism, and thereby of the unity we seek. In the first place, there was, and still is, a conception which ultimately derived from the liberal theology of the nineteenth century with its romantic undertones. Can the unity of Christians be achieved in a spiritual unity that would transcend the divergences of official formulations of faith? Is Christianity no more than an ethical attitude—the Golden Rule—that is expressed in different creeds reflecting diverse cultures? In this case, the differences would be superficial; they would reside in the sound of words, but not in the meaning and intentions expressed by the words. In final analysis, there would be, despite real divergences in creeds and dogmas, an authentic oneness in space and continuity in time of the

---

1. Gustave Thils, *La Théologie oecuménique. Notion—Formes—Démarches*, Louvain: Warny, 1960.
* Reprinted with minor alterations from *One in Christ*, 1979/1, p.11-20.

universal moral conscience, in which one could see the essence, not only of Christianity, but even of all religion. In the words of Auguste Sabatier, "in history Christianity offers itself to us as the end and the climax of the religious evolution of humankind."[2]

Such an idea is not far below the conscious level of much contemporary theological writing, especially in the attempts to find a congenial approach to the great non-Christian religions. It prolongs the broader romantic movement which entered theology through the central gate along with Schleiermacher's feeling of absolute dependence.[3] In its early form it influenced the Catholic school of Tübingen. In another form it dominated the Anglicanism of the Oxford movement, when John Henry Newman intellectualized it as the illative sense.[4] Theological romanticism fostered a method of analysis of religious feelings and attitudes that contributed to shape the Life and Work movement. In conjunction with the American theology of the social gospel,[5] it strengthened the belief that the implicit language of action and of life could eventually unite what is still separated by the explicit language of doctrine. Shared action would inspire a common experience and feeling, which some day would promote a new language in which Christians would unite their formulations of the faith. The romantic approach fostered the hope that a new experience of oneness in spite of differences will render previous theologies obsolete. But this was at a high cost, for it assumed that there may be legitimate dichotomies between feeling and intellect, language and thought, life and doctrine, deeds and thoughts. Such a dichotomy is unacceptable. A word—a "seme" in linguistic jargon—is a thought that is being formulated. An unspoken thought, a word that is not yet exteriorized, is not without language, for "thinking thought" (*la pensée pensante* of Maurice Blondel) gives birth to "thought thought" (*la pensée*

2. Auguste Sabatier, *Outline of a Philosophy of Religion Based on Psychology and History*, New York: Harper and Brothers, 1957, p. 133.

3. Friedrich Schleiermacher, *The Christian Faith*, Edinburgh: T. & T. Clark, 1956.

4. John Henry Newman, *Essay in aid of a Grammar of Assent*, Image Book edition, New York: Doubleday, 1955, ch. 9.

5. See Paul Minus, *Walter Rauschenbusch: American Reformer*, New York: World Publishing Company, 1988.

pensée[6]) through the mediation of the semantic systems placed at its disposal by language. A word is a sign whose significance is thought. Human experience knows no signification without a sign, no thought without a language. The conclusion is well expressed at the end of Wittgenstein's *Tractatus*: "What one cannot express one must leave unspoken."[7]

In the second place, simple institutional resistance made it necessary to try another approach. The structures of separated churches have an in-built interest not to allow reconciliation. They tend to prevent joint action from committing them too far, from inspiring truly common fellowship, and, where such common fellowship may already be experienced, from expressing itself openly in a joint credal statement. At an unofficial dialogue of Orthodox with Roman Catholics, I once heard Georges Florovsky say: "There is no ecumenical theology; there are theologies of ecumenism." This is precisely the question: Should ecumenism give rise to new theological languages, which eventually will formulate the traditional doctrines in new ways? Or should ecumenism find its voice only in the older languages of the long-lasting church institutions? In this alternative, one would have to conclude that if Orthodox, Catholic, Anglican, Lutheran, Protestant theological thought can formulate doctrines that are common, parallel and even convergent, they nevertheless cannot profess altogether isotopic doctrines. Ultimately, there would be as many kinds of ecumenisms as there are Christian Churches. There would not be one ecumenism that all could share. The curve of the ecumenical movement would remain asymptotic. The Christian Churches could get very close together, but never become organically one.

The agreed statements of the bilateral dialogues constitute a new kind of literature, which testifies to drastic changes in theological methodology. These texts are new as to their status, neither private nor fully official. It may not be necessary, however, to make a sharp distinction, in this growing library, between what is official and what is not. Official dialogues do not commit the churches involved until the churches'

---

6. Maurice Blondel, *La Pensée*, Paris: PUF, 1948, vol. I, p. 81-121; Blondel's view can be related to the early Greek Fathers' reflections on *Logos endiathetos* and *Logos prophorikos* in God.

7. "*Wovon man night sprechen kann, darüber muss man schweigen*" (*Tractatus logico-philosophicus*, n.7, in Ludwig Wittgenstein, *Werkausgabe*, vol. I, Frankfurt-am-Main: Suhrkamp, 1989, p.85).

authorities endorse their reports. The churches are nonetheless logically bound to take the agreements arrived at by their theologians in dialogue with other churches very seriously.

The leaders of the Catholic Church and the Anglican Communion who encouraged the dialogues were aware of the newness of this documentation. Not inadvertently did Pope Paul and Archbishop Michael Ramsey authorize the publication of the *Final Report* without endorsing its contents (the Windsor, Canterbury, and Venice statements[8]). This was totally new in the canonical practice of the Catholic Church. The authorization to publish was more than a bishop's *imprimatur*, which only indicates that the bishop finds a book exempt from doctrinal and moral error. It can be likened to a recommendation of good study material, worthy of careful attention from bishops, theologians, canonists, and the people of God in general.

Although not official, the agreed statements are not simply private, since official commissions have produced them. A careful reading of their content shows that they challenge classical theologies, traditional methods of theologizing and defining doctrines, the interpretation of some dogmatic positions, and even the very formulation of some doctrines. They witness to the contemporary ecumenical situation, which require the churches to be more aware of being challenged by Christ's prayer for the oneness of his disciples. They invite ecclesial authorities to listen to the suggestions made in these agreements. They consequently call the churches to seek to what extent the positions of the signers ought to become standard theological positions. They confront the churches with perspectives of reform, with profound modifications of habits of thought and of work, of life and of faith, especially where a long-lasting *status quo* has conveyed the impression of theological and doctrinal immutability.

These agreements are new also by their origin and by the way in which they have been composed. Bilateral dialogues seek how diverging traditions can be brought to converge. Such a convergence can only be the fruit of the adoption and the practice of a new theological language. Polemical approaches and apologetic arguments have to be overcome. When, at the beginning of the twentieth century, anti-Protestant apologetics gave way to anti-Modernist apologetics theology came to be centered on a

8. Text in *The Final Report*, London: CTS/SPCK; 1982.

search for arguments of credibility over against both historical criticism and the Modernist symbolic conception of dogma. By contrast, the trend of the bilateral agreements is to seek for authenticity, that is, fidelity to Scripture as to the norm that is itself its own norm[9], and to the central Christian tradition as transmission and interpretation of the gospel. Authenticity means rediscovering the meaning and value of faith through a new theological method. It is profoundly personal, yet radically objective. It is tied to history in the double sense of the events of the past and of historical involvement today. The bilateral dialogues lead the churches to a joint experience of Christian authenticity through mutual sharing.

The churches are urged by ecumenical dialogues to pass from a synchronic to a diachronic self-understanding. All churches have shown a dominant tendency to select one moment of their past and make it classical, to erect it as normative for future theologizing. This is not special to theology. It also happens in art and literature, when the academy selects norms of proper diction, spelling, grammar, style of writing, patterns of painting. It appears, however, that a school of thought which identifies strict Thomism or any other system as the final norm for theology cannot engage in fruitful dialogue. It can explain itself, respond to objections, formulate arguments. It can compare itself with other synchronic systems, such as Scotism, Lutheran orthodoxy, the theology of Jean Calvin or that of Richard Hooker, and then sort out similarities and differences. This, however, is not dialogue.

As already explained, dialogue presupposes an agreement to talk together *par cum pari*. Each side considers the other, at least hypothetically, as of equal value with itself. It agrees to try the other's formulation of faith or theology, to enter as deeply as possible into the mindset of the other side, a mindset which precisely makes another formulation of faith, another theology, possible, consistent and, in its own context and boundaries, faithful to the gospel. At the limit, each side agrees to consider the formulations of faith of the other as valid alternatives to its own. At this level, one is no longer in apologetics, or even in comparative theology. One is engaged in a process of convergence, in an attempt to build together a theology that will do justice to the history and the insights of both sides. Such a theology will be new in relation to all past theologies of the dialoguing churches.

---

9. The classical expression is *norma normans non normata*.

Dialogue obliges each side to adopt a very flexible view of the theology that serves as its own point of departure. Theology can no longer be a synchronic synthesis elaborated at what one would like to see as the high point of intellectual and spiritual development. Such a synchronic synthesis and other similar constructs become historical moments in an ongoing movement of which the present dialogue constitutes another moment. And the *kairos* of this precise moment resides in the opportunity to enrich one theological language with another, through modification of its paradigms, of its method, of its formulation of the Mystery in the light and with the help of the paradigms, the method, the formulations that are familiar to the Church with which one is dialoguing.

Seen in this light, the contemporary bilateral dialogues and their agreed statements acquire a further dimension. They posit a challenge to the classical methods of confessional theology done in the isolation of a particular tradition. This tradition may have believed itself to be essentially or exclusively faithful to the revealed word in the Bible. It may have believed itself to be the original Christian tradition from which others derived. It may have encompassed in itself a whole universe of culture. None of these claims, however, can deny the fact that theology has been done without the contribution of other traditions, and in some cases against them. Length and width of tradition, biblical purity, may indeed mitigate, but they cannot reduce to naught, the crippling effects of isolation.

It belongs to the nature of science, as today conceived and practiced, that to every hypothesis another may be opposed. Not only is applied research necessary, new basic research is also indispensable to the advancement of science. A language is scientific to the extent that it questions its own structures, methods, and axioms. It is moreover generally accepted, in the linguistic school deriving from Ferdinand de Saussure[10], that meaning is not found in the terms or words used, but in the relationships between them. While it is not relative as opposed to absolute, meaning is relational. This is true both of the structure of each language and of the comparison of languages. Because of their existing relationships natural languages are grouped into families according to their formulations

10. Ferdinand de Saussure, *Cours de linguistique générale*, Paris: Payot, 1971.

and expressions of basic aspects of human nature and culture, as for instance in the Indo-European (Sanskrit, Greek, Latin, etc.) or the Semitic (Hebrew, Aramaic, Arabic, Syriac, Maltese, etc.) groups of languages.

The way to enrich a theology—both a theological system devised by individuals or schools, and the basic doctrinal orientations of each Christian church—is by learning another. This other theology or doctrine can then act as a counterhypothesis, a foil to test one's spontaneous assumptions or reasoned convictions. It can lead to the realization that one's inherited or chosen formulations of faith have lacked a dimension that another tradition has appropriated or has better developed. Then, each of the main streams of the Christian tradition will come to see itself as a moment, be it an important one, in the on-going diachrony of Christian doctrine. It will learn, perhaps slowly, to revise its doctrines and dogmas, because at no time and in no form can the Christian faith be constituted as a total and final synchrony. There is no doctrine today that can be said to have arrived at its ultimate formulation. The perspective is not that the participants in ecumenical dialogue ought to change sides. Rather, they should together build a valid alternative to their own cherished positions.

In 1972 the Anglican-Roman Catholic Conversations in the USA issued a short methodological statement, with the aim of determining the conditions for a proper ecumenical dialogue[11]. Six principles were highlighted as of special importance: (1) There is a "paradoxical tension" between revelation and its theological expression. (2) "Contextual transfer" may be necessary from one language to another. (3) The "emphasis" given to doctrinal definitions is "relative" to their cultural importance. (4) "Doctrinal pluralism" may be needed to do justice to the Mystery. (5) We should appraise the teachings of other Churches with "empathetic evaluation". (6) "Responsive listening" ought to mark our dialogues.

The crucial principle is the second, contextual transfer. The point is not only that "a Christian today, in order to be orthodox and to maintain continuity with the tradition expressed in the language of another day, may need to find new language and even new concepts to express the same truth." From the point of view of theology as language one should go further. Ecumenical dialogue requires

---

11. Text in *Called to Full Unity*, p. 57-60; *Documents on Anglican Roman-Catholic Relations II*, Washington: USCC Publications, 1973, p. 49-53.

learning theological languages other than one's own. Yet one cannot really know a language just by looking at its grammar. Only as one appropriates its thought-forms can one speak it. Learning is for the purpose of speaking, and one does not speak without thinking. The conditions for an ecumenical dialogue can therefore be put in sharper form.

The primordial condition is to be willing to have one's theology and doctrine questioned. One need not expect aggressive attacks, but the mere fact of accepting to grant another Christian tradition the parity demanded by the *par cum pari* principle implies taking other formulations of faith and theology as possibly equivalent to one's own, as at least provisionally valid alternatives. Such equivalence is not a concordism of different confessions, credal statements, or theologies. It implies attempting to think and live with other categories of thought, other models of imagination, other styles of Faith and Order and of Life and Work. It means trying to speak another theological language.

The outcome of such an attempt should not be returning to one's old theology after making an interesting experiment. This is indeed a very natural temptation. If I return to my older methods and formulas, confirmed in my previous belief that these were the best and the truest, I probably show that my real purpose in dialoguing was not to reach the fruits of dialogue, but to try out another kind of apologetics. The aim should rather be the perfecting of new theological models, enriched with the insights of other traditions. I suspect that if this were seriously done, joint theologies, joint formulations of faith would soon render institutional separations obsolete and intolerable.

If one thing is clear from the agreements that have been issued on Eucharistic faith, it is that the major Christian traditions can now speak the same sacramental language. This was emphasized in the Lima document of the Faith and Order Commission (1962). It may not yet be quite the case in regard to ministry, although the dialogues of the Catholic Church with the Anglican Communion, with the Lutheran World Federation, with the World Methodist Council, have underlined a growing convergence. In 1973, the *Canterbury Statement* on priesthood and ministry treated the topic more empirically than theologically, and it did not entirely harmonize two conceptions of the ministry: In n.13 the priesthood is essentially related to the High Priesthood of Christ, while most other sections are descriptive of the priesthood as pastoral ministry. Nevertheless, the statement conveyed the convictions that no ultimate differences oppose Anglicans and Catholics on the nature of the priesthood.

Likewise, in 1970, the Catholic participants in *Lutherans and Catholics in Dialogue IV* suggested, without affirming it, that Lutheran Orders could be recognized by the Catholic Church in their fidelity to the gospel and their validity[12]. This suggestion implies the conclusion that whatever differences still exist between Lutherans and Catholics are minor, compared to their fundamental agreement. In other words, I recognize the language of my partners in dialogue as Catholic language; and I hope that they recognize my language, at this moment of its diachrony, though not necessarily in the past, as in some sense Anglican language or Lutheran language.

From this point of view, the problem that faces the dialogues, as they sharpen their approach to the vexing question of infallibility, is the most crucial that they can possibly confront. To speak a new language at this point amounts for Catholics to admit that the language of Vatican Council I on the infallibility of the bishop of Rome speaking *ex cathedra* is already obsolete. It requires recognizing that the concept of infallibility was contextually relevant during a relatively short period of the church's history. This concept developed slowly between the Gregorian reform and the nineteenth century, was officially adopted in 1870 and, within one hundred years of its adoption, had already lost much of its meaning. Further, there is considerable uncertainty as to what a new language can be at this point, because some of the alternatives—uncertainty in faith, eschatological indefectibility—seem at first sight unsatisfactory. In these conditions, institutional resistance to change may disguise itself as defense of confessional orthodoxy. This may well take the form of a new apologetics for papal infallibility; and the slight advances of Vatican II over Vatican I on this question could possibly be used to this end. Were this the case, the dialogue would risk being caught in a seesaw, what has been accepted with the right hand being withdrawn with the left. What seems to have been received at one moment of the dialogue may be ignored or denied at a later moment. Critical convictions—such as the impermanence of all language—may be passed over lightly in the final redaction or interpretation of a statement.

---

12. *Lutherans and Catholics in Dialogue IV. Eucharist and Ministry*, Washington: USCC Publications Office, 1970, n. 54, p. 31-32.

❦

A frequent structure of the statements that have been made by Lutherans and Catholics in Dialogue includes a common chapter and two reflective chapters representing the Lutheran and the Catholic viewpoints. What is said in common runs the risk of being undermined by blatant or hidden apologetics in Catholic or Lutheran reflections. The way out of the ensuing dilemma is, however, if not simple, at least clear. It consists in asking myself, as a Catholic, how I could express in Lutheran language what I understand the Catholic doctrine to mean. Thus, infallibility has something to do with certainty in teaching. Because one cannot teach what is not formulated, the church must be able to formulate its faith with the certainty of being true to the revelation. What Vatican Council I added with the definition of papal infallibility was simply that in certain conditions and circumstances there can be an antecedent conviction that what the bishop of Rome will define will be true and, by implication, will have the shape of irreformable doctrine.

One point follows. If certainty in teaching and in formulating doctrine can be expressed in Lutheran language, the antecedent certainty about definitions *ex cathedra*, that was dear to Pius IX, need not belong to the basic model of Catholic language, even though the specific circumstances of the nineteenth century made it appear as a quasi-necessity. The ongoing diachrony of theology and ecclesiology may possibly show it to have become dysfunctional.

Approaching the ecumenical dialogues with the linguistic status of theology in mind would help overcome the remaining hurdles. If this proves impossible, if dialogues are eventually unable to build a constructive model for the formulation of doctrine with certainty that could replace the infallibility model, then the partners in dialogue will have engaged in comparative study without being able to negotiate the passage to dialogical theology. They will have fossilized synchronic structures of their confessional traditions without entering the moving terrain of the diachrony which, sooner or later, overcomes all intellectual constructs. This may, of course, be the best one can do in certain sets of circumstances. Yet a determined theology of dialogue should aim further and higher. It should attempt to find a more encompassing model for the formulation of Christian truth than the infallibility model, or the Lutheran confessional model, or the Anglican doxological model.

❦

After it mentioned the parity demanded by ecumenical dialogue, the decree *Unitatis redintegratio* added, in Austin Flannery's translation: "From such dialogue will emerge still more clearly what the situation of the Catholic Church really is[13]." The word, situation, translates the Latin, *condicio*. Does *condicio* refer to the situation of the Catholic Church in relation to others, as the translation suggests, or rather to the internal condition and development of the Church and its teaching? Comparing one's language with other Christian languages helps to discover the exact nature and the inner structure of one's own and the value of what is said in it. N.11 of the decree asserts that there is a "hierarchy of truths" in Catholic doctrine, "since these truths vary in their relation to the foundation of the Christian faith." The foundation (*fundamentum*) is no other than the Christological center of faith. Or, in a more exact formulation, the Word, eternal, incarnate, risen, looms behind all Christian theological languages as their common metalanguage.

Ecumenical dialogue tests our languages until we discover together which of their semantic and grammatical forms are the more transparent to the Word, which of their mythical constructs are the more effective in letting us, hearers and speakers, discern the Word and speak it.

---

13. "*Ex tali dialogo etiam clarius innotescet quae sit revera Ecclesiae catholicae condicio*" (Austin Flannery, ed.: *The Documents of Vatican II*, New York, 1975, p. 461)

CHAPTER 4

SEARCHING FOR LANGUAGE

Ecumenism is essentially a search for a new theological language. One can even say that the central ecumenical question is this: How can two traditions that have grown apart over five centuries arrive at a common theological language? The bilateral agreements illustrate this search for a new theological language. Language is not a haphazard construct. It falls within certain fairly definite patterns. The disappointing experience of artificial languages like Esperanto or Ivo shows that languages cannot be invented. They grow out of definite cultural conditions. The history of Latin suggests that one cannot artificially keep a language alive. By contrast, the resurgence of dead languages, such as Hebrew in Israel, was made possible by the emergence of a cultural environment that required new forms to be introduced, a vocabulary to be modernized, obsolete or complicated aspects of grammar to be updated or simplified. The problem of a new theological language is not unlike that of spoken languages.

A structural approach to language emphasizes three fundamental dimensions. Language is paradigmatic in semantics, syntagmatic in grammar, mythic in its attempt to express the absolute and the universal. The paradigmatic dimension provides basic tools of thought and communication, namely the phonemes or significant units of sound. The syntagmatic dimension gives the means to combine these tools in recognizably meaningful ways. The mythic dimension establishes symbolic conventions expressive of experiences of ultimacy in a given culture.

Theology itself has the form of a language. It uses a certain number of units of religious meaning in keeping with the revelation or tradition to which it relates. It unites these notions in the syntagmatic synthesis of a creed according to the analogy of faith, in keeping with the inherent logic of each theology. It finally places this synthesis, whether completed or, more often, attempted, at the service of a higher goal that corresponds to the experience of grace. One cannot determine which of these three dimensions is primary, since they are intrinsically inter-related. In no language do semantics and syntax exist apart from each other. In theological language no concept or creed is without a reference to an experience of ultimacy. The proper task of theology is to formulate systematically and specifically what the general mythic dimension of language conveys spontaneously and generically, namely the power of the word (small w) to express the Word (capital W), the possibility of speaking to communicate, not only the daily happenings, needs, and purposes of empirical life, but also the convictions, hopes, and insights that are born from experiences of transcendence.

Looking at the threefoldness of theological language as a whole, it also appears that two points of view are relevant, synchronic and diachronic. In synchrony, a language is taken as it stands at a given moment of time. In diachrony, it is studied in its development over a determined period. Thus one can study English as, for instance, spoken in Wales in 1920. One can also trace the evolution of Eng-lish from Shakespeare to Faulkner. As language about God, theol-ogy too can be examined at specific moments of its development. A coherent synthesis that has taken shape in a specific time and place may then appear to transcend time. The theology of Thomas Aquinas forms a whole, which remains the same today as it was in the *Summa Theologica* when Thomas died. One may, or may not, find this synthesis adequate to contemporary experience. If one finds it adequate, however, one is dispensed from the need to look for a better theology.

Theological languages can also be studied in the making. Then one does not look at a finished system, but at a complex evolving model, some aspects of which become dysfunctional with time. The-ology never ceases readjusting itself, modifying its units of meaning, altering its overarching points of view as it discards or improves upon older methods of argumentation, ever attuning itself to new insights into its own past and to the experiences of living men and women, and anticipating further developments which the signs of the times may call for.

❧

In this perspective the question of Christian unity must be faced at another level that than of feeling as an interior impression. Neither the

Church nor theology judge what remains purely interior to conscience. This canonical axiom well corresponds to the linguistic requirement of thought. If unity is recognizable from the use of a common language, this is because there is no unity without communication, and the prime medium of human communication is language. The question of Christian unity has therefore to be faced at the level of doctrines and institutions, and not only of feelings. But doctrines do not exist outside of their formulations. Theology, *theologia*, has to be *logia* in order to be *logia* about God.

Theology is a concrete, existential activity of reflection in the framework of the Christian faith. It arises from faith seeking to develop its insight into the object of faith, God revealing himself. It is therefore not really useful to define theology in the abstract, with a degree of generalization that would cover all its manifestations through all ages. A theology needs to be defined in relation to the horizon that has nurtured it. This horizon is primarily the Church as a community of believers united by a common faith in the revelation of God through Jesus Christ. It is also the world in which the Church lives and tries to announce the gospel.

This context rules out of theology merely rational or philosophical endeavors, which, however careful they may be in their inventory of data and their logic, do not take the profession of faith as their basis and starting point. It also rules out speculative elaborations that would attempt to reach an extra-temporal coherence obtained once for all and valid for all times and places. If, with Bernard Lonergan, one calls this the classicist view, then no theology has ever been fully classicist. All theologies reflect some type of historical-mindedness, in that they share their contemporary mindset, and history has seen many mindsets come and go. Within the historical context of the period and culture in which they live, theologians work at a very concrete task of reflection in the Christian faith. Reflection has the basic and ultimate purpose of reaching insights into the subject matter of its attention.

The direction of research, the tools, the hypotheses are for a large part provided by the dominant concerns and the state of intellectual sophistication of each age. In this broad cultural horizon theologians find material that will be correlated and given coherence by the insights they will obtain. There is rarely a mere borrowing from the contemporary culture, for the relationship of theology to its secular horizon is often antagonistic. In any case, it is in the horizon of their world that theologians find the horizon of their thought. This is no other than what they have assimilated of remembered history and contemporary experience.

The Christian past gave birth to successive kinds of theologies, which coincided with the time of the Fathers, the Middle Ages and the Byzantine era, the Reformation and the beginning of the modern age, the nineteenth century and the scientific age, until finally the twentieth century saw the first signs of an ecumenical theology. Borrowing and modifying St. Anselm's famous phrase[1], one may characterize these theologies as *fides quaerens anagogiam, fides quaerens analogiam, fides quaerens historiam*, which, in broad approximation, correspond with the first three types of theology. After the parenthesis of the polemics and apologetics of the counterreformation, a fourth type occurred, *fides quaerens rationem humanam*. This type of theology came to an end with the overcoming of scientism by the further scientific and philosophical developments of the twentieth century. And there is today a general sense that a new theological age is dawning. Can it be characterized? Lonergan has spoken of the passage from classicism to historical-mindedness, Gregory Baum of the Blondelian shift[2]. Karl Heim and Thomas Torrance, in different ways, have connected theological method with scientific awareness[3]. Other thinkers have expressed the thought that a historic period has ended, the Protestant era for Paul Tillich[4], the *Neunzeit* for Romano Guardini[5], the counterreformation for many Catholics in the wake of Vatican Council II. The task is to foresee in what direction theology will go, after what sort of insight it will strive, to what sort of synthesis it may arrive.

---

1. For brevity's sake I refrain from raising the question of the theological status of religious reflection in other religions.

2. *Fides quarens intellectum* was St. Anselm's paraphrase for theology (*S. Anselmi opera omnia*, vol. I, Edinburgh: Thomas Nelson, 1946, p. 94).

3. Gregory Baum, *The Credibility of the Church*, New York: Herder and Herder, 1968, p. 12-15.

4. Bernard Lonergan, *Method in Theology*, New York: Herder and Herder, 1972, p. 326; Gregory Baum, *The Credibility of the Church*, New York: Herder and Herder, 1968, p. 13-15; Karl Heim, *Christian Faith and Natural Science*, Gloucester, MA: Peter Smith, 1971; Thomas Torrance, *Theological Science*, London; Oxford University Press, 1969.

5. Paul Tillich, *The Protestant Era*, Chicago: Chicago University Press, 1948, p. 222-233.

In my book of 1975, *La Théologie parmi les sciences humaines*[6], I indicated what still seems to me a fruitful direction. The central argument was that, since theology, whatever else may be said about it, is always, in John Macquarrie's term, God-talk[7], it should have its proper place among the sciences of human language. Beneath all the forms that theology has taken and may take, one fact remains constant: Theology always starts from religious discourse, from the use of language to speak about God and to God. It begins in human talk about God in explanation and proclamation, and human talk to God in worship and prayer. It is a systematic study of this God-language. A first level, underlying all theology, corresponds to the classical description of mystical theology as the record of the human experience of God. Explanation and proclamation explain and proclaim what has been sensed of the self-revelation of God in Christ through the Holy Spirit who enlightens the hearts of the faithful. A second level, that of theology as such, corresponds to the more scholarly but less immediate study of criteria and symbols of the Christian experience. On the relations between these two levels, I share the judgment of Dom Illtyd Trethowan: "Dogmatic theology, properly understood, articulates mystical theology, which has as its content the experience of faith in developed, matured form[8]."

Theology is necessarily couched in language. It is in language that we think. And in order to be able to think new thoughts about new things we develop new languages, as can be seen in the sciences that have emerged since the end of the eighteenth century. Each science is a language. It is also in language that, as soon as we wish to communicate our insights, we express ourselves, acquiring, adapting, inventing symbols, and combining them together in recognizable patterns of coherence. Just like natural languages, technical languages function according to two basic dimensions. They use a certain number of linguistic symbols (semantics) and they relate these symbols together so that meaning can emerge from them (syntax). As a technical language, theology should be approached in the same way. Its structure is linguistic. Its task is not

---

6. Romano Guardini, *Das Ende der Neizeit. Ein Versuch zur Orientierung*, Würzburg: Werbund-Verlag, 1951.

7. *La Théologie parmi les sciences humaines. De la méthode en théologie*, Paris: Beauchesne, 1975.

8. John Macquarrie, *God-Talk. An Examination of the Language and Logic of Theology*, New York: Seabury Press, 1979.

essentially different from that of any language, namely, to reach and to express insights. What specifies it as God-language is that these insights relate to the experience of God rather than to empirical problems of living or to a multitude of scientific and artistic occupations.

A further description of the theological task would say that theology speaks about God and investigates the conditions of this speaking, which evidently cannot be done without using language as the chief medium of thought and expression. This tautology has at least the advantage of showing that theology always has a linguistic status, whether its practitioners are aware of it or not. All theologies need to elaborate their method. In all theological methods certain theological paradigms—units of theological meaning—are combined according to certain syntagmatic rules. The primary task of theology is to identify these rules, to construct its linguistic structure. Admittedly—*fabricando faber;*—this need not precede talking about God, although a linguistic structure (*la langue*) underlies God-talk (*la parole*), as a metalanguage underlies a language.

It is on purpose that I have called language the chief medium, rather than the only medium, of theology, for I would not rule out other possible media[9]. A theology can be expressed in several semiotic systems, if these systems are able to give form to insights related to the experience of God. One can make a good case for a theology of icons, in which the rules and conventions of icon-painting provide certain units of theological meaning which, being put together syntactically by the artist within the grammar of the craft, communicate religious meaning. Likewise, Gothic art may be seen as a theology using architecture and the related crafts as its means of expression. The late Paul Evdokimov saw in this sort of thing a theology of beauty[10]. I would rather see beauty as a virtual dimension of all theology, and characterize artistic theologies as theologies couched in visual non-linguistic semiotics. What makes them theological is not the medium, but the semiotic capacity of the medium as applied to the experience of God.

Even there, however, language remains necessary. One cannot explain an icon or a cathedral without using language to exfoliate the theological use of the artist's medium of expression. What gives language a po-

---

9. Illtyd Trethowan, *Mysticism and Theology. An Essay in Christian Metaphysics*, London: Geoffrey Chapman, 1975, p. 79.

10. See Appendix: "Can Theology be non-verbal?"

tentially theological dimension is not the fact that it combines certain vocal noises in a certain order, but that, in combining phonemes, it creates a semiotic system through which thought is formed, meaning is expressed and recognized, communication takes place, even with ups and downs in both eagerness and effectiveness. Because it creates symbols, language is more than the warning systems used by animals. It expresses meaning, judgment, understanding, and not only feeling. It gives shape to the understanding that I reach and communicates it. It transmutes personal inner understandings into interpersonal exchanges and social constructs. The profound social entelechy inscribed in the structure of thought is such that one does not think without using language inwardly, and that the language one thinks with is the very same language that one speaks. A similar social entelechy pertains to the linguistic structure of theology.

This social dimension draws attention to a further aspect of religious language, that of myth-making. All human cultures have myths, in which, among other subject matters, they have expressed their perception of their prehistoric origins. In this sense they have a connection with history, even when the details of the past have been absorbed by a tendency to universalize the lessons they convey. The events they narrate are both temporal and permanent. They thus posit various moments at which eternity cuts through time. Myth is therefore essentially religious, and all religious language has a mythical dimension. Besides the paradigmatic and syntagmatic dimensions of its basic structure, the combination of which conveys meaning, language therefore has a third dimension without which one could speak neither about ultimate reality nor about anything with ultimate concern. The mythical dimension of ultimacy opens up when the speaker tries to convey a meaning that utterly transcends the selves of both speaker and listener. The speaker then initiates a process of myth-building. A myth, in this sense, is a discourse that tries to convey the universal meaning of a local event, or the eternal meaning of a temporal event. Myth-making differentiates religious and theological language from both empirical and scientific languages, and reveals a mythopoetic dimension of faith[11]. It follows that demythologizing as a theological enterprise is a contradiction in

11. Paul Evdokimov, *L'Art de l'icône: théologie de la beauté*, Paris: Desclée de Brouwer, 1972.

terms if it means more than attempting to explain the meaning of religious myths. A more exact description of the theological task would say that it should preserve, enrich, proclaim, and explain the mythical import of the Christian message. One may find confirmation of this analysis in the otherwise puzzling fact that at the very moment when demythologization of the Scriptures canalized theological reflection, a remythologization was taking place in some of the liberation theologies which, for better or for worse, incorporated the Marxist myth of future freedom in their discourse. This three-dimensional approach to theology as language points to a task to be done in relation to the mythical dimension of religious language.

Anthropologists have paid special attention to the sundry forms of ancient myths. The Christian myth that we call salvation history, however, may well be the key to the meaning of all mythology, since it includes the theology of God's inner life, the act and purpose of creation, the economy of the incarnation of the Second Person, and the lengthy return of all things to God through the inspiration of the Third Person. This slow pilgrimage to God is precisely where human history fits. Not only the Christian myth as a whole, however, needs to be investigated in a new key. The hermeneutical task also requires interpretation of the language of Scripture and of the traditions that derive from it, with all available means, including structural linguistics and its extensions in semiotics and in discourse-analysis.

The writers of the conciliar decree, *Unitatis redintegratio*, deliberately discarded, as the title of chapter I, the expression, "Principles of Catholic ecumenism," in order to use the other expression, "Catholic principles of ecumenism." During the preparatory phase of the council, *De ecumenismo catholico* was the name of a subcommission within the Secretariat for the Unity of Christians. This subcommission worked at a project for a directory of ecumenism. The expression, "Catholic ecumenism," was used as a subtitle in this projected directory. It appeared in the title, *De ecumenismi catholici principiis*, of the first chapter of the schema *De oecumenismo* that was distributed to the council fathers in May of 1963. In the second redaction, however, distributed in 1964, the title had been changed to *De catholicis oecumenismi principiis*. Thus the redactors wished to assert the oneness of ecumenism. There is only one Christian world, which ecumenism hopes to gather into one *ecclesia*.

The point of departure for such a reintegration has to be the contemporary pluralism of the languages of faith and of theology. The problem is not how to streamline theologies into one. It is to discover the oneness of faith within the pluralism of doctrines and theologies. One cannot therefore separate, even though one has to distinguish, the diverse and many Christian Churches and communities. Likewise, one cannot separate, although one must distinguish, Christianity and Judaism as the biblical way of salvation. Ecumenism must work in all directions as it seeks to identify the semiotic level of faith, which underlies the discordant languages of doctrine. And if there is no such semiotic level, or if this semiotic level is discovered to be itself diverse, then the ecumenical task is to arrive at a metalanguage, which, by pointing out the oneness of faith in a new way, should allow the formation of theological languages that will be mutually comprehensible even if they have to remain different.

How can one arrive at this metalanguage? One must distinguish two phases. In the first place, a phase of mutual comprehension is elementary and indispensable. A Catholic has to understand the sense of Luther's formulations of justification by faith before arriving at an agreement with Lutheranism. The conciliar decree insists on this (n.9). It points to the urgency of this phase of the dialogue with Protestantism in four areas to be investigated in common: the confession of Jesus Christ (n.20), the study of Scripture (n.21), the sacraments (n.22), the Christian existence (n.23). In the history of the ecumenical movement this corresponds fairly well to the purpose and the method of *Faith and Order* before the Lund meeting of 1952. This method, often called comparative ecclesiology, enabled the participants to make headway in mutual understanding. Due no doubt to the fact that the Secretariat for the Unity of Christians was building on the previous experience of Faith and Order, the dialogue recommended by the council goes further, for one can compare without dialoguing, and the council placed dialogue at the center of ecumenism (UR. n.4). It described its nature as grounded in the parity of the dialogants[12], which should be a parity of both competence and position. Although the formulations of creeds, dogmas and doctrines from which the dialogants start may be divergent

---

12. See my book, *Juana Inès de la Cruz and the Theology of Beauty* (University of Notre Dame Press, 1991), pp. 208-213.

and even opposed, their connexions with the revelation in Christ are considered, at least hypothetically, as equivalent. This is precisely what constitutes parity of dialogue: One recognizes the language of the other as a possible expression of the metalanguage of Revelation. The purpose of dialogue is then to discover in what way and to what depth one can enter in the intentionality of this language, analyze its value, gauge its validity, share it, incorporate it in one's own ways of speaking, thinking, seeing, living, and eventually use it as one's language.

This first phase of dialogue leads to a second. Mutual understanding opens up common discovery and elaboration. In the light of the meta-language that has been uncovered beneath the diversity of theological languages among those involved in dialogue, the possibility emerges of a common language, which, compared to all the languages previously in use, will be new. Ultimately, this second phase of dialogue should arrive at a new formulation of the faith, in which, through the *renovatio ecclesiae*, the *interior conversio*, the *novitas mentis* (newness of mind) that are asked for in n.6 and 8 of *Unitatis redintegratio*, all partners in dialogue will be able to recognize, in their unity with others, a development of their specific tradition. The ultimate purpose of dialogue is to learn a semiotic that will be new in relation to all older symbolic systems, Catholicism and Orthodoxy as well as Protestantism, yet in which continuity with the past will be recognized by all.

If this conception is not explicitly formulated in the texts of Vatican Council II, some documents from the Holy See have followed the same direction. So did Paul VI's encyclical *Ecclesiam suam*. The pope presented dialogue, *colloquium*, as mutual listening, it in the perspective of the world and what was to become the constitution *Gaudium et spes*. in the perspective of divided Christianity and what was to be the decree *Unitatis redintegratio*. On 21 November of the same year the conciliar decree on ecumenism was issued. Describing the purpose of dialogue as a "deeper knowledge and a clearer manifestation of the inexhaustible riches of Christ," it oriented ecumenism toward the elaboration of new theologies. Along the same lines the Secretariat for the Unity of Christians declared on 15 August 1970:

> The partners will work together towards a constructive synthesis, in such a way that every legitimate contribution is made use of, in a joint research aimed at the complete assimilation of the revealed datum. This research involves an effort to return to the sources, going back

to Christian origins before the appearance of subsequent disagreements. It also calls for an effort at discovery, looking to the future for solution that will transcend present historical differences[13].

The intent of the council was thus interpreted in a prospective direction, turned toward the future, toward new solutions to be reached through a new theological and doctrinal language.

The bilateral dialogues try to discover a language that can be shared by the two traditions involved. There is no theoretical reason why this could not be done by more than two dialogue partners. Yet one multiplies problems by multiplying the languages to be compared, evaluated, and eventually merged into a new language. In this new theological language the Churches should eventually find the main lines of a new doctrinal language for normative doctrines. The Churches are thus entering the process of discovering a fruitful metalanguage. Catholics have known for a long time that within the Catholic Church the metalanguage of one faith underlies a pluralism of rites and theologies. There now appears that beneath the divergences between Churches there also exists a metalanguage, the perception of which should lead the Churches to find an adequate structure for their common language of the future. This situation may be interpreted in two ways.

Firstly, divergences in the doctrinal languages of the Churches are assigned to the same level as the divergences of theological languages. In this case, Catholicism, let us say, would be a theology; Anglicanism would be another one, their metalanguage being the Christian faith. This, however, may not do justice to the depth and violence of past confrontations. Furthermore, the most thorough differences among the participants in ecumenical dialogue do not always coincide with Church affiliations. There already are common theological languages that cross the boundaries of the Churches. Secondly, Church languages affect the very substance of faith. Christians have been separated, not only by ways of thinking and speaking, by models that they have erected and verified or failed to verify, but also, as the opposing traditions of the Reformation and the Counter-Reformation contended, by diverging confessions of faith. Is there a metalanguage that can paradoxically unite or reconcile doctrines of faith that are not isotopic, remain mu-

---

13. ... *ubi unusquisque par cum pari agat* (*Unitatis redintegration*, n.9).

tually incomprehensible, and cannot be reformulated in the terms of the other Christian traditions? Only one answer seems possible. If the metalinguistic level that unites diverse theologies within one Church cannot be other than its doctrine of faith, the level beyond this, which serves as metalinguistic ground of the doctrines of faith of the Christian world, cannot be other than the revealing act of God, the revelation in the active sense of the term. Only through a thorough *resourcement* can a common language of faith be spoken by diverse Churches.

The problem confronted ARCIC-I from the beginning: How can two traditions that have grown apart over five centuries arrive at a common theological language? The statements of Windsor, Canterbury, and Venice established basic structures for such a language. Even if "new and serious obstacles" to reunion have arisen since their publication, the formula of the Windsor agreement remains valid: "We are convinced that if there are any remaining points of disagreement, they can be resolved on the principles here established[14]."

---

14. "Reflections and Suggestions concerning Ecumenical Dialogue," V, 2, c (The Secretariat for Promoting Christian Unity. *Information Service*, n. 12, December 1970/IV, p. 9).

CHAPTER 5

SPEAKING TOGETHER

The major characteristic of the ecumenical movement in the 1970's was the existence and work of the bilateral dialogues. Before the council dialogues between theologians of two Churches had indeed taken place. There had been approaches, suggestions on possible paths to reunion, exchanges of views and discussions. In the sixteenth century, the Regensburg Colloquy (April-July 1541), in the seventeenth century the correspondence between Leibnitz and Bossuet, in the twentieth century the Malines conversations were notable precedents. The first failed because rejected in both Rome and Wittenberg. The others did not attempt to arrive at a joint position. Quite other have been a number of recent ecumenical statements, fruits of the sort of dialogue that was recommended by the decree *Unitatis redintegratio*. The present chapter will survey the purpose and scope of some of these statements, and look at the methodology of the participants.

The brief under which the Anglican-Roman Catholic International Conversations (RCIC-I) met was formulated in the *Malta Report* of January 1968, which was composed by a Preparatory Commission set up by Pope Paul VI and the archbishop of Canterbury, Michael Ramsey. The *Malta Report* attested that there exists an identity of faith between the Catholic Church and the Anglican Communion (n.3), and that divergences derive "not so much from the substance of this inheritance as from our separate ways of receiving it" (n.4). It recommended that "we should examine further and together both the way in which we assent to and apprehend dogmatic truths and the legitimate means of understanding and interpreting them theologically" (n.5). Several lines of convergence were indicated (n.6). Although it is not stated as such in the report, the "separate ways of receiving" our common inheritance have something to do with our formulations of the faith. Assent to and apprehension of dogmatic truths are related to the language of theological speculations and doctrinal confessions. As explained in the pervious chapter, the problem faced by the bilateral dialogues can therefore be pinpointed as a problem of language. Two Churches that seek reconciliation need to speak the same language in order, precisely, to speak together, for no one has yet found a way to speak together in different languages.

The general purpose of the agreed statements was well indicated when the *Malta Report* listed a number of topics for conversation between the two Churches. Besides "the way in which we assent to and apprehend dogmatic truths and the legitimate means of understanding and interpreting them theologically" (n.5), it mentioned "the nature of the priesthood and the meaning to be attached... to the word, validity" (n.19), "the nature of authority with particular reference to its bearing on the interpretation of the historic faith to which both our Communions are committed" (n.20). The International Commission that was created in 1969 to implement the broad project of the Preparatory Commission began by studying the recommendations of Malta. Granted that, in the present state of divided Christianity, immediate reunion between any two Churches was not possible, the only alternative was "reunion by steps and stages". Between Anglicans and Catholics the first important stage should be a review of the doctrinal grounds of the divisions of the sixteenth century, which were hardened by polemical theologies in the seventeenth and eighteenth.

Since, in the case of Anglicanism and Catholicism, one is dealing, not with religious movements, schools of theology, philanthropic societies, or mystical chapels, but with Churches—Pope Paul even spoke of sister-Churches—the basic questions refer to the doctrines that are properly constitutive of a Christian Church, namely, the Eucharist and the ministry. It is a principle inherited from the Church Fathers that the Eucharist is the basis and the center of the community, which is the Church. Without the Eucharist there may be a community of faith united by a common concern for the Word of God, but there would not be, in the words of Paul, "a communion in the blood of Christ... a communion in the body of Christ..." (1 Cor, 10:16). It is essentially when the communities gather to worship the Father through the Lord Incarnate that the faithful experience themselves to be the Church. The Eucharist is not merely a fraternal meal. It is "the supper of our Lord", in which the Lord feeds us with the fruits of his sacrifice. The structural identity between the Church's Eucharist and that of the

Lord is embodied also in the minister who presides liturgically at the Supper. The doctrines of the Eucharist and of the ministry must therefore constitute the cornerstone of any Catholic agreement, in keeping with points 3 and 4 of the Lambeth Quadrilateral[1].

In this ecclesial perspective, ARCIC-I identified its own achievement as an "agreement on essential points of eucharistic doctrine"..., in which "nothing essential has been omitted." The "intention was to reach a consensus at the level of faith.[2]" The conclusion was far-reaching: "We believe that we have reached substantial agreement on the doctrine of the Eucharist" (n.12). Again, as they introduced the Canterbury statement, the co-chairs wrote: "We believe that in what we have said here both Anglicans and Roman Catholics will recognize their own faith." The statement itself professed to "seek to express our basic agreement in the doctrinal areas that have been the source of controversy between us, in the wider context of our common convictions about the ministry" (n.1). It concluded: "What we have to say represents the consensus of the Commission on essential matters where it considers that doctrine admits no divergence." It had reached consensus "on questions where agreement is indispensable to unity" (n. 17)

The Venice statement on authority in the Church, of September 1976, was more modest in its affirmation: The consensus reached, it stated, "covers a wide area" (preface). "Our degree of agreement... argues for greater communion between our Churches" (ditto). "We believe that this Statement on Authority in the Church represents a significant convergence with far-reaching consequences" (n.25). The conclusion spoke of an "agreement on the doctrines of authority, apart from the qualifications of n.24". These qualifications referred to Anglican reservations regarding the interpretation of the Petrine texts of the New Testament, the language of *jus divinum* used at Vatican Council I, the affirmation of papal infallibility, and the attribution of universal immediate jurisdiction to the bishop of Rome. While the Commission was cautious in assessing the level of its consensus, it remained forceful as it summed up the method it has used since its inception:

---

1. J. Robert Wright, ed., *Quadrilateral at One Hundred*, Cincinnati: Forward Movement Publications, 1988, p. vii.

2. Co-chairs' introduction to the *Windsor Statement*, in *The Final Report*, London: CTSA/ SPCK, 1982, p.11. .

In our three Agreed Statements we have endeavored to get behind the opposed and entrenched positions of past controversies. We have tried to reassess what are the real issues to be resolved. We have often deliberately avoided the vocabulary of past polemics, not with any intention of evading the real difficulties that provoked them, but because the emotive associations of such language have often obscured the truth (n.25).

These expressions conveyed the conviction that a consensus had been reached, and that henceforth the ARCIC statements could be used in both communions to formulate the faith and transmit the two Churches' doctrinal heritage. ARCIC-I held that it had brought to light the metalanguage that underlies the faith expressed in the doctrines, and experienced in the liturgies of the communions involved.

The *Canterbury Statement* on Ministry (1973) carefully delimited the scope of its agreement: "Our intention has been to seek a deeper understanding of Ministry which is consonant with biblical teaching and with the traditions of our common inheritance, and to express in this document the consensus we have reached" (n.1). The consensus, however, may seem to be undermined by the fact that the text presents two theologies of the ministry that it did not harmonize perfectly. Most of the document envisions ministry in terms of *episcope*, oversight, understood as spiritual leadership of the community in the doctrinal, liturgical, and social areas. Meanwhile, n.13 justifies the task of *episcope*, not by the sociological necessity of giving a head to the community, but by the intrinsic symbolism of the Eucharistic assembly. Hence the critical questions: Does the Christian ministry derive from a sociological law of social bonding in religious societies? Or does it embody a function that is implied in the symbolic structure of the Eucharistic? Or is it, perhaps, both?

If the Canterbury statement used two languages, respectively focused on episcopal oversight and on Eucharistic sacramentalism, and formulated two theologies of ministry, these theologies remained within recognizable reach of each other. The two languages are mutually understandable. Two models describe the nature of the ministry, in the hope that those who favor the one over the other will nonetheless recognize both as proportionally isomorphic. It follows that they ought to lead to a point where each tradition can recognize a legitimate continuity with its ministerial structures and its theological understanding of them. This is precisely the meaning of "substantial agreement" as ARCIC-I used the expression.

When it bears on the Eucharistic experience of the presence of the Lord in its sacrificial reality as the body of Christ offered for the sins of the world, doctrinal agreement must be more than a theological conclusion or inference. It must be a consensus in faith, for it directly touches the heart of the Christian revelation, even though the specific forms of ministry, as they developed and varied through the ages may have been due to practical necessity, to sociological opportunity, no less than to theological congruence. By the same token, a consensus of faith in regard to the Eucharist or the ministry is to be placed at the center of what Vatican Council II called the "hierarchy of truths" of the Catholic faith (UR. n.11). True doctrines do not all stand in identical relationship to their Christological center. Their nearness to the Word of God incarnate, who died and rose again for our redemption, determines their place in the hierarchy of truths. Once agreement has been reached on the center itself, agreement on the periphery ought to follow. In other words, a consensus on the Eucharist, confirmed by agreement on the ministry, implies a fundamental convergence on the nature and structure of the Church as the community of salvation.

ARCIC-I did not define its method. There was nonetheless a strong hint, in the *Malta Report*, about the proper structure of the coming dialogue: "Divergences since the sixteenth century have arisen not so much from the substance of our inheritance as from our separate ways of-receiving it" (n.4). The basic methodological principle was therefore to try together to receive, understand, and transmit our common inheritance while eschewing the polemical language of the past. Language is more than words. The way we speak determines the structure of our thought. To speak a polemical language means that we think polemically. If one does not wish to think polemically, one needs to find and to speak another language. To Anglicans and Roman Catholics such a language is fortunately available, for they have both inherited the languages of Scripture and of the Church Fathers, especially, but not only, that of St. Augustine. To the extent that Anglicans read their classics, they hear from Richard Hooker (1554-1600) a theological language that was largely inspired by Thomas Aquinas.

The option of ARCIC-I comes through clearly in the Windsor and Canterbury statements. In Scripture read in the light of the patristic tradition it found what it called "our common inheritance". It was in line with this choice that the Windsor statement reduced to a footnote such an important, but more recent, and controverted development as the doctrine of transubstantiation. Likewise the Canterbury statement abstained from the Anglican debate whether episcopacy is of the Church's *esse* or the *bene esse*. Nor did it discuss the exact relationship between bishops and priests, a question on which several schools of thought were alive and well in Catholic theology at least until Vatican Council II.

This focus on the biblical and patristic language was paired with another methodological principle. ARCIC-I intended to look at the two communions and their doctrines as they are today, in their synchrony in the context of the modern world, and not only in the diachrony of their separated histories. This was relatively easy for Eucharistic doctrine, the main lines of which are clear in the early Church and already in the New Testament. It was not so easy with the doctrine of ministry. The successive forms and the progressive understandings of the ministry that emerged in the many centuries since it began make it impossible to understand ministry apart from its history. The challenge was to look synchronically, in our times and with modern concerns, at a radically diachronic reality of the Church's life. The answer consisted in bringing the synchronic or synthetic point of view and understanding of the ministry, formulated in n.13 of the Canterbury statement, under the light of the diachronic or historical development described in the preceding sections (n.3-12). The historical development of the ministry, as *episcope* of the People of God, is cut through by a cross-section (n.13), which reveals the inner structure of ministry as *hierateuma* (priesthood) ordained to the *anamnesis* (the liturgical remembrance) of Christ's words and deeds.

In the matter of authority it was necessary to use a bifocal approach, taking account both of the evangelical nature of authority in the People of God, and of the historically changing forms of this authority at its main periods of development. One cannot say, with some critics of the Venice statement, that its topic was "who has authority" rather than the nature of authority. The topic was indeed the nature of Christian authority, examined, however, not as a theoretical question, but in the concrete forms of its embodiment in certain organs and persons. Viewed from this angle, Christian authority emerges as being essentially conciliar and collegial. It exists and functions by virtue of the *koinonia* of the disciples and for this *koinonia*.

The universal Church itself is a *koinonia* of Churches. Historical description and analysis go together with, and are guided by, theological reflection on the requirements of authority when it is informed by commitment to Christ and by trust that the spirit of Christ will assist its conciliar function of "excluding what is erroneous[3]."

The ambition of Lutherans and Catholics in Dialogue has been far more modest than that of ARCIC-I. This American Commission wished from the beginning to be a group of scholars doing theological reflection together, rather than a pioneering team somehow striving to commit the Churches to its conclusions. From 1965 to 1995 Catholics and Lutherans published nine joint statements: *The Eucharist as Sacrifice* (1967), *Eucharist and Ministry* (1970), *Papal Primacy* (1974), *Teaching Authority and Papal Infallibility* (1979), *Justification by faith* (1985), *The One Mediator, the Saints, and Mary* (1992), *Scripture and Tradition* (1995). These statements express a common faith where this is appropriate. They also attempt to break new theological ground and to suggest possibilities for future convergence. Speaking to the academic community in the Churches they carefully document all that they say, and they are not afraid to confront controversial questions. By the same token, their conclusions are at times tentative, proposed and submitted rather than magisterially asserted. This explains the frequent practice of this dialogue of dividing its statements in three sections: A common section is to be read in the light of the specific problems and prejudices of each side that are then examined in two separate sections. Because this commission intended to do solid theological work, it published most of the background papers discussed by the group. It also commissioned two notable exegetical investigations by an ecumenical team, on *Peter in the New Testament* (1973) and *Mary in the New Testament* (1978). With intellectual honesty it drew attention to persisting disagreements. In a word, its joint statements were meant to be used as tools for study rather than as expressions of faith.

At the international level, the Lutheran-Roman Catholic Joint Commission has produced several notable reports: *The Gospel and the Church* (Malta, 1971), *The Eucharist* (1978), *Facing unity* (1985),

3. *Authority in the Church I*, 1976, n.19 (*The Final Report*, p. 82).

Church and Justification (1994). The first of these remained very general. It centered its approach on the question of Justification, in the light of which it looked at "the Gospel", "the ministerial office", "papal primacy", and "intercommunion." Perhaps because the program was too ambitious, three Catholics and one Lutheran disagreed with parts of the report and added their own qualifications. The second report offered a comprehensive treatment of eucharistic doctrine approached from a Trinitarian starting point, for "the mystery of faith" is experienced "through, with and in Christ, in the unity of the Holy Spirit," for the "glorification of the Father" and for "the life of the world". The text made ample use of previous ecumenical documents[4]. It is marred, however, by an apparent discrepancy between part I (Joint Witness), where transubstantiation—without the term—is affirmed by both sides (n.22), and part II (Common Tasks), where the use of the term in Catholic doctrine is listed among "controverted positions" (n.49). On the whole, these two documents, while interesting and useful, are far from groundbreaking. They provide views of the past rather than outlooks on the future. In its later projects, *Facing Unity*, and *Church and Justification*, the Joint Commission became more creative, and it anticipated the work of the unofficial group, *Oekumenische Arbeitsgemeinsshaft*, which initiated the movement that led to the Joint Declaration of October 30, 1999.

It would be too long at this point, and possibly superfluous, to outline the sequence of ideas in the many statements that have issued from all the bilateral dialogues and from some other, unofficial, dialogues. The work of the Roman Catholic, Presbyterian and Reformed Consultation, although less substantial than that of Lutherans and Catholics in Conversation, and less ambitious than ARCIC in terms of purpose and method, deserves study with its statements on *Ministry in the Church* (1970), and *The Unity we Seek* (1977).

More weighty, however, is the work of the *Groupe des Dombes*, an unofficial dialogue that has been in existence since 1937. It includes Lutherans and Reformed on the Protestant side. It is highly

---

4. Notably, the *Windsor Statement* of ARCIC, the document of the *Groupe des Dombes*, *Vers une même foi eucharistique* (1972), the USA Catholic-Lutheran statements, and several documents from the Faith and Order Commission of the World Council of Churches.

regarded in French-speaking countries as a gauge of the present state of ecumenical reflection. In its early years, this group did not publish statements and simply outlined a few "propositions." Later, like the official dialogues, it issued full-sized documents: *Toward a Common Eucharistic Faith* (1972); *For a Reconciliation of Ministries* (1973); *The Episcopal Ministry* (1976); *The Holy Spirit, the Church, and the Sacraments* (1979); *The Ministry of Communion in the Church Universal* (1985); *For the Conversion of the Churches* (1991), *Mary in the plan of God and the Communion of Saints*[5] (part I: In history and Scripture, 1997; part II: Controversy and conversion, 1998). The *Groupe des Dombes* followed the same sequence of topics as the dialogues of Catholics with Anglicans and with Lutherans: from the Eucharist to the ministry to various aspects of the Church. It spends as much time as seems useful discussing each question, and feels no urgency to produce a statement. Unlike *Lutherans and Catholics*, however, some of its statements have been presented in an avowedly unfinished state, in the hope that they might feed a broader ecumenical reflection.

To what extent should the bilateral dialogues be broadened so to engage other groups, or theologians in the Churches at large, or the academic and ecclesial communities? One can put the question differently: Should the bilateral commissions rewrite their statements in the light of the critiques of their work that have been formulated? Should they gradually improve their statements, so as eventually to give them a definitive form based on a broad discussion in the theological community?

The *Groupe des Dombes* has produced successive versions of some of its agreements. A brief history of the group published in 1964[6] included several sets of theses unanimously accepted by the participants between 1956 and 1962. Some, on original sin (1956), on the Church (1958, 1960), did not directly anticipate the agreed statements. Others, on ministry (1957), on pastoral authority (1959), on the priesthood (1961 and 1962), served as first drafts for more complete statements composed in the 1970s. More to the point perhaps,

5. English translation: *Mary in the Plan of God and in the Communion of Saints*, New York: Paulist Press, 1999.

6. *Dialogue oecuménique*, Taizé: Presses de Taizé, 1964; English version: Patrick Roger, ed., *Ecumenical Dialogue in Europe*, Richmond, VA: John Knox Press, 1966.

it is not unusual for the Faith and Order Commission of the World Council of Churches to provide successive editions of one document. Thus the statement on "a mutually recognized ministry" (Accra, 1975) grew from a previous version presented in 1971 in Louvain. Both ARCIC and *Lutherans and Catholics in Dialogue*, however, decided against the principle of rewriting its texts. Their documents express the consensus of the participants at a given date. They illustrate the state of ecumenical convergence at a particular point in time, even if their ultimate purpose—to act as theological catalysts in and between the Churches—is not universally successful.

In spite of this, ARCIC-I was sufficiently impressed by some criticisms to formulate answers to them at its Salisbury meeting in January 1979. These *Elucidations* are substantially a response to critics of the Windsor and Canterbury statements. The points selected for reply underline sensitive areas of the statements that provoked critical reactions. In the Windsor statement these were the concept of *anamnesis*, the notion of "becoming" as expressing the relation of bread and wine to the sacramental Body and Blood of Christ, the role of faith in the reception of the sacrament, the practice of eucharistic reservation. In the Canterbury statement they were: the priesthood as an analogical reality, the sacramentality of ordination, the origins of the ministry, the ordination of women, and the problem of Anglican Orders. By and large, the Salisbury *Elucidations* did not add anything of substance to the findings of Windsor and Canterbury. They reiterated the conviction that the methodology of ARCIC was correct, and that the scope of its previous statements amounted to an agreement at the level of faith concerning the Eucharist and the ministry. One may wonder in any case if answering critics is the best method to arrive at a universal consensus. It might be better to finish a select project, and then to look at criticism as a whole rather than to give piecemeal answers to specific points. I am not aware that other bilateral groups have tried to engage in a dialogue with their critics.

A few Anglican Evangelicals aimed a different kind of critique at ARCIC-I. The agreements, they said, are not really to the point. For the question today remains what it was at the time of the Reformation: What are the nature and the means of Justification? Before Evangelicals can truly find value in the agreed statements—so the reasoning goes—they must be convinced that the Catholic Church does teach and practice Justification by faith, and not the Justification by works of the later Middle Ages, against which Luther and the Reformers rightly reacted. This is not the forum to decide if the later Middle Ages truly taught Justification by works, or if Anglican theology should look for models among the Fathers of the Church rather than in Lutheranism, or yet in what measure the traditional comprehensiveness of Anglicanism can accommodate opposite concerns and methods. Yet the Evangelicals made an important point. Whatever one may think of Justification by faith in the polemics of the Reformation, the agreements of Anglicans and Catholics must be seen on the background of the Reformation divide. If one may hope for a reunion of Anglicans and Catholics, one should never forget that oneness is total or it is not. Their reconciliation by stages should itself be a stage in the reconciliation of all Christians. That some of the concerns of the continental Reformation are also found within the Anglican Communion should make one particularly sensitive to the importance of the doctrinal Reformation for the task of Christian reconciliation. It is only in faith, and not by works, that Christians can be reconciled, even if there is work to be done by way of dialogue.

Two questions that have not been formally treated in most dialogues involving the Catholic Church have now become unavoidable.

Firstly, should the *Final Report* of ARCIC-I and the subsequent reports of ARCIC-II justify lifting the canonical obstacle to Eucharistic sharing? This question is all the more painful as in sacramental theology most Churches and communities of the West do not draw the same conclusion as the Orthodox and Catholic Churches from their ecumenical principles. These two Churches regard Eucharistic communion and ecclesial communion as strictly correlative. To decide that Eucharistic communion may be shared among members of two Churches presupposes that each Church has recognized the other as truly an embodiment of the Church of Christ. In this case the practice of "inter-communion" becomes a simple matter of discipline, which is to be decided with the proper caution by the responsible authorities in each Church. In the decree on ecumenism, n.8, Vatican Council II recognized the value of a desire for intercommunion based on the hope to become one. Because of the importance of this desire for each believer and for the future of the Churches, it reserved the relevant decision to "episcopal authority" in each diocese, unless a more general ruling has come from a National Conference of Bishops or from the Holy See. While this illustrate remarkable progress compared with the harsh regulations of the code of canon law of 1917, a theological hurdle still stands: When should a bishop judge that the goods to be obtained from holy communion ought to prevail over the scandal of separation between the communities involved? As a matter of principle, Eucharistic communion should not be far from ecclesial communion. Before reaching the stage of regular Eucharistic sharing one ought to pass through the stage of explicit Church-recognition. Nevertheless, since baptismal unity necessarily entails an orientation toward Eucharistic unity, it is itself not complete where Eucharistic hospitality is not practiced. The actual sharing of spiritual goods ought to be set by the degree of unity that already exists. There should be room, however, for the anticipation of full ecclesial communion through an occasional experience of Eucharistic unity. This ought to be sufficient today to justify the practice of inter-communion for the proper spiritual and ecumenical reasons.

Secondly, a problem of recognition of ministry was made acutely painful by the condemnation of Anglican Orders, in 1896, by Leo XIII, long before the Catholic concern for the unity of Christians had entered the ecumenical stage. This brings us back to the methodology of ARCIC-I. To abstain from the polemics of the past means, among other things, not to enter the disputes that provoked, and that followed, the apostolic letter of Leo XIII, *Apostolicae curae*. ARCIC-I avoided facing the historical problem of Anglican Ordinations at the time of the Elizabethan settlement, which had been the focus of Leo XIII's letter. Meanwhile, a remarkable development occurred in Rome, when popes Paul VI and John Paul II did not hesitate to welcome bishops of the Anglican Communion in ways that would make no sense if they did not implicitly regard these prelates as truly bishops in the Church of Christ. Thus a new climate for mutual assessment has been created at the highest levels of the Churches. ARC-USA brought attention to this in its statement of 1994, "Anglican Orders. A report on the evolving context of their evaluation in the Roman Catholic Church[7]."

The canonical category of validity no longer provides, if it ever did, an acceptable standard to describe and evaluate the sacramental expe-

---

7. Common *Witness to the Gospel. Documents on Anglican-Roman Catholic Relations*, 1983-1995, Washington: USCC, 1997, p.125-148.

rience of other Churches than one's own[8]. In this sense, the Windsor and Canterbury statements saw Anglican ordinations in a horizon that could not have been seen by Leo XIII. Whenever this new context is more fully acknowledged and more richly furnished, one will need to implement the logical consequences for sacramental theology. This will not be in terms of validity, unless one intends, once again, to revive the polemics of the past.

---

8. See my book, *A Review of Anglican Orders. The Problem and the Solution*, Collegeville, MN: The Liturgical Press, 1991; and my paper, "*Apostolicae curae* and the snares of tradition", in R. William Franklin, ed., *Anglican Orders. Essays on the Centenary of Apostolicae curae, 1896-1996*, Harrisburg: Morehouse, 1996, p.30-47.

CHAPTER 6

FOR AN ECUMENICAL ECCLESIOLOGY

The preface of *The Final Report* identified the notion of communion as the ecclesiological key to its findings. The nature and role of communion in the ecumenical context were further developed by ARCIC-II in *Church as Communion* (1991). Similarly, after it surveyed possible models for reunion (*Facing Unity*, 1985),) the international Lutheran-Catholic Joint Commission identified the purpose of its work as "*koinonia* founded in the Trinity" (*Church and Justification*, 1994). Likewise, the dialogue between the Catholic Church and the World Methodist Council, in 1986, presented "*Towards a Statement on the Church*," where it declared *koinonia* to be more important than any particular model of Church union" (n.23). In 1992 also, delegates of the Catholic Church and the Church of the Disciples published a joint study of the "Church as Communion in Christ."

Two major points emerge from the concentration of bilateral dialogues on the Church. Firstly, the question of the structure of the Church as it relates to ministry is of major importance. Ecclesial structures are not simply matters of organization. They are closely related to the discipline of the sacraments, which itself derives from doctrinal understandings of the nature and purpose of the Church and its ministry. Secondly, the understanding and the experience of the Church as *koinonia* provide the proper context for an eventual solution of traditional differences among Christians regarding structures of ministry, ordination, and the episcopate.

In these conditions, the first step to take in order to advance the dialogue further should be to examine the extent and the way in which the Scriptures provide light on the nature of ministry, on ecclesial structures, and on the Church as *koinonia*. In keeping with the preface of *The Final Report*, however, it seems logical to begin with *koinonia*, and hence to look at structures. In so doing one should keep in mind that the various readings of Scripture regarding the institutional aspects of the Church were themselves nurtured in diverging doctrinal traditions and practices of government. The interpretation of Scripture is not only a starting point. It constantly nourishes theological constructions at all levels of speculative thought. And it cannot avoid being itself affected and transformed by hypotheses and by theses in search of demonstration. In the framework of the *triplex munus* of Christ, the major differences between Christian communities of faith do not relate to the participation of the People of God in Christ as Prophet (following the Spirit: LG 12), but to their participation in Christ as Priest (offering the sacrifice of praise: LG 10) and as King (organizing society: LG 31).

The New Testament alludes to multiple images of the Church. Vatican II listed the sheepfold, the flock, the field of God, the vineyard, the house of God, the tent (tabernacle), the household and dwelling-place of God, the heavenly Jerusalem, the bride of the Lamb, the Mother, the People of God, the New Israel (LG. 6-7). It went on to emphasize the image of the People of God. In the ecumenical dialogues that ensued, however, the consensus has been growing that the dominant image should be *koinonia*.

It is chiefly in the Pauline corpus, notably in Romans and the neo-Pauline letters to the Colossians and the Ephesians, and in Luke's Acts of the Apostles that the Church is presented as the communion of the disciples in Christ. The Church of God, which was originally called into being through Moses during the Hebrews' wanderings in the desert on the way to Mt. Sinai, was reconstructed in the death and rising of Christ. God's eternal purpose, already at work in the gift of Torah to the people of Israel, was achieved in Jesus Christ and through his Spirit. Restored as the Church of the risen Christ, the "assembly of God" is recognizable wherever the Apostles and their associates and successors in the task of ministry preach the "gospel of God". Unlike the Old Israel, the Church of the risen Lord is open to the Gentiles, who, when they come to believe in Christ and receive baptism, are grafted on the original tree of Israel (Rom. 11,16-24). This universal dimension of the Church of salvation was revealed to Paul on the way to Damascus, and also, as Luke also recorded it, to Peter in the house of the centurion Cornelius (Acts 10).

The Pauline principle tallies with the description of the primitive Church by Luke: "There were only one heart and one mind of the multitude of the believers..." (Acts 4,32). Indeed various problems emerged as the Christian Church grew, notably concerning the status of

Gentile-Christians in relation to Torah, and, by implication, concerning all Christians' allegiance to and interpretation of the Law. It was the purpose of Luke to show that the early difficulties between Jews and Gentiles, Judeo-Christians and Gentile-Christians, were smoothed over in a spirit of communion, on the basis of an awareness and conviction of responsibility for one another in the oneness of the body of Christ.

As the gathering of true believers for worship and fellowship in their several communities in towns and homes, the Church is many. The experience of communion, which is comparable with the union of husband and wife, which the Epistle to the Ephesians sees as a paradigm of the Christian Church, unites the two dimensions of the one and the more than one inseparably. As the body of Christ in mystery, or mystical body, the Church is one. It is part of what Paul also calls "the mystery of his will..." (Eph. 1,9), that was hidden in God and has now been revealed. There is only one mystery, of which the Church is both the expression and the experience.

In the Acts of the Apostles *koinonia* holds the key to the solution of the basic problem of the one and the many—Jews and Gentiles in one Church, -, and of the ensuing questions concerning the relevance of Torah for Christian life. All other problems stirred by the coexistence of one and many can be solved on the same basis: one bishop and a multitude of people, one humanity and two sexes, one faith and numerous cultures, one Church and many nations.

In the community of the Church the New Testament ascribed a unique place to the Twelve. It also acknowledged the existence of a group that was called "the brothers of the Lord." One of these, James, presided over the community in Jerusalem. There was also a wider group of missionary Apostles, among them Paul, Barnabas, and, arguably, several women who acted as Paul's coworkers, such as Phoebe, "our sister, who is deaconess of the Church in Cenchrae" (Rom. 16,1), Prisca, wife of Aquila, Paul's collaborators (Rom. 16,3), Junia, who was Paul's relative and whom he said to be "noble among the Apostles" (Rom. 16,7). In the Johannine writings "the beloved disciple" occupies a special place. After sitting next to Jesus at the Last Supper (John 13,23), he led group of communities that are known through the Epistles of John. Another special place is that of Mary Magdalen, who was, according to the gospel of John, the first ocular witness of the resurrection (John 20,1-18).

All in all, the Pauline corpus and the Acts mention a number of offices or ministries that structure the life of the communities, yet without dwelling on the distinctive functions of each. There are *presbyteroi, episcopoi,* who may be identical, prophets, deacons, *didaskaloi* (teachers), administrators. Some among them receive an imposition of hands: thus Paul from Ananias (Acts 9:17), Barnabas and Paul from the "prophets and doctors" of Antioch (Acts 13,1-3), Timothy from Paul (2 Tim.1,6). They are thus "set apart" for a mission (Acts 13,2). The New Testament, however, does not pose the question whether these missions and ministries belong, like Christian discipleship, among the constitutive features of the community. Paul finds a guiding principle for their relationships in the Greek parable of the feet and the body: All must function in harmony. Harmony or unanimity is clearly at the heart of the Church as *koinonia.*

It is on this background that the place of Peter in the New Testament ought to be seen. The synoptic gospels give Peter the first place among the Twelve. Paul accepted this, even when he stood up to rebuke Peter for his ambiguous attitude regarding the fellowship of Judeo-Christians with Gentile-Christians (Gal. 2,14). Peter's prominence was also recognized in the Gospel of Luke. This prominence was a responsibility to "comfort his brethren" (Luke 22,32), though the brethren are not identified further: Are they the Apostles, or all the believers? And it is hazardous to argue that Peter's prominence in the New Testament was intended to continue through a *Peter redivivus* mystically acting through his successors in a universal primacy. The identification of the bishops of Rome as Peter's successors and the inheritors of his primacy came much later than the New Testament, and can be traced to other sources.

At least one point is clear in the New Testament. Many developments in organization occurred in the first centuries, regarding the mono-episcopal structure of a diocese, the presbyteral group of the bishop's co-ministers, the close ties between bishop and deacons, the preeminence of some episcopal sees over others, partly in keeping with the political status of the cities where they are located, partly because this city housed the relics of a prominent Apostle, and of two in the case of Rome -. All ministries, however, remained at the service of the fundamental communion of all the disciples of Christ. Ministry is for communion, not communion for ministry.

The late Jean-Marie Tillard did considerable work on the ecclesiology of communion. He showed that this was the predominant conception of the Church in the first centuries. He identified it as the key to the traditional conception of ministries, to the understanding of the Church as visible institution, and of the function of the bishop of Rome. He naturally concluded that it should remain at the center of Catholic ecclesiology. As Catholicism often sees the universal first and the local second, and Orthodoxy often does the opposite, an ecclesiology of communion overcomes the possible antagonism of these two points of view. Neither is the local Church a mere subdivision of the universal Church, nor is the universal Church the sum total of local Churches. Local and universal are fundamentally identical. The total Church is both local and universal, since all communities of believers exist in Christ by the power of the Spirit. This is particularly evident in a Eucharistic ecclesiology, for which the Church is constituted as the gathering of the faithful around the Eucharist. A Eucharistic celebration is always local, whatever the scope of responsibility of its presiding officer. There is then no more in the universal Church than in the local Church. The local Church is not under, though it is within, the universal Church. The whole Church of Christ is present and active (*subsistit*) in the reality of the local Church as the Church of God in a given place. In this sense the local Church is always potentially universal. Its universality should be manifest in manifold connections with other local Churches and with the ministerial and magisterial instruments that are at the service of catholicity, namely the episcopal College and the bishop of Rome as successor in the Petrine ministry. Classical Lutheran theology was aware of this broad patristic consensus on *communio*-ecclesiology when it referred to a *consensus quinquesaecularis* as a rule of thumb that set boundaries to the period in which the teaching of Christian doctrine was fully identical with the authentic tradition embodied in Scripture and confessed in the creeds. In regard to the nature of the Church as well as to other doctrines, however, the tradition seen as whole must imply both synchronic and diachronic unanimity. Through the Trinitarian and Christological controversies of the fourth and following centuries, the Fathers learned to agree, not only synchronically, with their contemporaries who held the same doctrine, but also diachronically, through time, as they considered normative the dogmatic decisions of the councils of Nicaea, Constantinople, Ephesus, and Chalcedon.

Doctrine receives its ecclesial norm from unity in time, whatever the intervening centuries and their controversies, with the consensus of the great patristic councils.

Scripture is inseparable from tradition. Yet fidelity to the great councils has been colored by a multitude of liturgical, homiletic, literary, and cultural practices and customs in which the faith and piety of the faithful have found expression. Here again harmony between the one (tradition) and the many (traditions) is at stake. There may be manifest harmony and cohesion. The many, however, may also be mutually incompatible. To the extent that one faith has found local expression in diverse customs, its unity may be placed in jeopardy by its enculturation in the many. The Scriptures constitute one whole, which is nonetheless crisscrossed by many trends of thought and many paths. Likewise, the tradition, one in its totality, abounds in disparate details and diverging movements. Conflicts have been frequent between the one and the many, unity and diversity, oneness and plurality, a common heritage and divergent initiatives. The history of the Church cannot avoid recording a basic tension between synchrony and diachrony. The harmony that has been reached in the specific circumstances of one period cannot possibly remain constant as it is assaulted by many forces that are unleashed by the passing of time, and as the conditions that presided over its formation deteriorate, die, and give way to new sets of circumstances.

Thus it came about that bishops in their governance of Churches, and theologians in their ecclesiological reflections, often forgot the centrality of the *communio*-ecclesiology that had dominated the patristic age. They often failed to give it the first place in their descriptions of the Church and in their relations with fellow believers. With the influx of Germanic tribes into the Church, the sense of a universal *koinonia* tended to diminish in the very process by which the gospel found expression in cultures that were only remotely connected, if at all, with the Jewish matrix of Christianity or with the nurturing atmosphere of the helleno-latin culture of the Roman Empire. While the patristic sense of the Church as *koinonia* lasted into the Byzantine theology of the continuing Empire in the East, the emerging Western nations gave shape to more diversified, and by the same token, smaller and less universal types – *typoi*—of the Church. Though they were one in faith, the Roman and the Celtic Churches differed widely in discipline, organization, and liturgy. The relative uniformity that ensued the adoption of Roman customs by the Celts, as endorsed by the synod of Whitby (664), did not slow down the diversification of Hispanic, Gallic, and Germanic Christian cultures. The further unification of customs that was achieved by Charlemagne in the new Empire of the Franks could not abolish differences in local Churches that had to face a multitude of new problems. Rivalries arose between metropolitans and bishops (instrumental in the forgeries of the False Decretals in the middle of the ninth century), between bishops and bishops over ownership of land and the right of patronage to chapels and Churches, between primates and metropolitans, between metropolitans and the bishops of Rome.

The disruptions caused by Norman incursions, first on the coast, and then inland along the deeper rivers, added political misunderstandings to doctrinal disagreements between Northerners and Southerners. In the controversy of the ninth century over predestination in France, southern bishops were more alert than northern bishops to the dangers of semi-Pelagianism. There were conflicts between clerics and lay lords, and appeals to Rome often became the only resource of beleaguered bishops against the incursions of lay power in their dioceses. Frictions were caused by local or regional discrepancies in knowledge of conciliar decrees, by the cost of obtaining and copying canonical and theological manuscripts, by the spread of inauthentic documents attributed to this or that father, pope, or council, and by the emergence of new theologies to fill the gaps that were opened by the increasing Western ignorance of the Greek language.

Ecclesiology was profoundly affected by these happenings. On the one hand, the sense of being one Church of East and West vanished. On the other, the relations of bishops with metropolitans, and of both with the bishop of Rome, introduced a new view of ecclesial hierarchy in the West, and thus caused further differences between East and West. This is not the place to rehearse the development of papal authority in the direction of universal immediate jurisdiction and of infallible authority in defining doctrine. The authoritative magisterium that the bishops of Rome acquired through the Middle Ages in Western Christendom tended to undermine, not only the authority of metropolitans, of regional primates, and of national synods, but also the sense of a universal *communio* among the Churches. The very resistance of the temporal power to papal sovereignty, as in the Pragmatic Sanction of Charles VII of France (1438), succeeded in restraining papal power in the short run. Except where the king, like Henry VIII of England, was not averse to shedding blood, it also had the unintended effect, over the years, of strengthening the determination of the bishops of Rome to preserve and exercise their power, and eventually to reserve the nomination of all Latin bishops.

In these conditions it is by no means surprising that in the turmoil of the sixteenth century new accents in ecclesiology streamlined some of the previous differences and over-stressed others. The rivalry between national Churches (the many) and Rome (the one) grew into a rejection of papal authority on one side, and a reinforcement of this authority on the other. Drawing on Martin Luther's insight regarding the foundational centrality of the gospel as the good news of justification by faith alone through Christ alone, the Confession of Augsburg described the Church as "the gathering of all the faithful, in which the pure Gospel is preached and the holy sacraments are properly administered" (art. VII). And if, in *Institutio christiana*, Calvin insisted that the Church is the mother of the faithful, who has nurtured them in the faith, he also emphasized that the Church is properly experienced as the community in which the testimony of the Spirit is normative for the discernment of Scripture. Meanwhile, fighting these orientations, Cardinal Bellarmine set the framework for the next three centuries of Counterreformation ecclesiology when he defined the Church as a perfect society that is as visible as the republic of Venice. In one direction, the sense of the communion of all Christians favored the internal and invisible, yet profoundly real, communion of the faithful with Christ over against its institutional aspects. In the other direction, the Church's institutional hierarchic government gained the upper hand over all ideal views of the Church as an internal and ultimately invisible spiritual gift. This movement reached its apex in the definition of papal infallibility at Vatican Council I.

In both directions the full sense of *koinonia* was overlaid with more peripheral concerns. In Protestantism the sense of communion in a visible universal Church was gradually replaced by fellowship in denominational Churches that were delimited by doctrinal lines and national boundaries. Meanwhile, Counterreformation Catholicism tended to isolate the Church's structure from the spiritual dimension of faith, moral theology from dogmatic theology, canon law from spiritual experience, this being turned over to the art of spiritual direction and to the literature of mystical theology. In the nineteenth century the popes attempted to correct this trend by issuing encyclicals on piety and especially on devotion to the

Virgin Mary. In twentieth century Catholicism, Pius XII made a more serious attempt to correct the balance by promoting an ecclesiology of the Mystical Body (encyclical *Mystici corporis*, 1943). Vatican Council II went further toward a recovery of the full ecclesiological tradition with its constitution *Lumen gentium*.

In spite of the problems and difficulties that I have noted in the history of ecclesiology, nothing in this overview suggests that it is not possible to delineate a minimal ecclesiology that should be at the same time sufficient and necessary for the reconciliation of Churches. The obstacles, however, are serious.

In the first place, one should be careful to do justice to divergent interpretations of the New Testament, Catholic and Protestant, which all claim fidelity to the scriptural sources. The alternative, that one of two broad strands of biblical interpretation simply gives way to the other, does not seem likely. Even though there is little, if any, difference today in historical-critical exegesis by Catholic and by Protestant scholars, differences emerge in the passage from scriptural analysis to theological construction. While many Catholic theologians differ in their use of conciliar decrees and papal statements and in their assessment of the authority of each, they all recognize a positive function to the magisterium, within the tradition by which the gospel is handed on from age to age. As a result, Catholic theology conveys the impression of being less biblical than its Protestant counterpart. Or else it looks profoundly biblical, as a number of papal encyclicals do, but at the cost of following an allegorical method of reading Scripture that is generally obsolete.

Within Protestant theology, however, other principles than the biblical text and its meaning are also at work. In Lutheranism, justification by faith has an indispensable methodological and metatheological role in the determination of Christian discipline, the formation of the Christian conscience, the elaboration of theological syntheses, and the evaluation of doctrines. In classical Calvinism, a central role is recognized to the testimony of the Holy Spirit in the heart of the faithful. In Orthodoxy, fidelity to the patristic consensus as conveyed through Byzantine theology and experienced in the Holy Liturgy functions as the supreme norm of Christian life and thought.

How problematic may be any attempt to harmonize such diverse methodological axioms is easily seen, if one considers the primacy of the bishop of Rome as it was described by Vatican Council I. To an intrinsic principle of authority the Counterreformation joined, if not opposed, an extrinsic principle, the authority of the bishop of Rome as presiding head of the Episcopal College. In the period of the Reformation the followers of Luther and those of the pope were both well aware of the problem: Can the written Word of God in Scripture truly be the ultimate norm (*sola Scriptura*) of Christian doctrine, if the spoken word of the Church's supreme episcopal *magisterium* is the proximate norm? Is the existence of an unquestionable extrinsic authority—whether the bishop of Rome, or the Sorbonne, or the consensus of universities and theologians—compatible with the model of an intrinsic norm of doctrine, whether this is intrinsic to Scripture, to tradition, or to the conscience of believers? All sides in the sixteenth century affirmed the existence of a "gospel in the heart" that is in full harmony with Scripture. They could not agree, however, on its normative function over against institutional guarantees and guarantors of orthodoxy. One may naturally wonder if contemporary Christians are in a better position to agree, after the encyclicals *Humani generis* of Pius XII (1950), *Humanae vitae* of Paul VI (1968), and *Splendor veritatis* of John Paul II (1993). Yet positions that seem solidly anchored in official teaching in one period may be corrected later. Even in Catholicism a principle of historical relativity is at work, since it is not rare for the teaching of one pope to be corrected by one of his successors or by a council. The decree on Religious freedom (*Dignitatis humanae*) of Vatican Council II contradicted all the popes of the nineteenth century. *Unitatis redintegratio* departed from the stance of Benedict XV and Pius XI on the ecumenical movement. The constitution *Lumen gentium* corrected the ecclesiology of the Counterreformation and completed that of Pius XII.

One can never learn too much wisdom from those who know. The basic problem of contemporary Catholicism is not that through their encyclicals the bishops of Rome try to guide the faithful in their day by day, or at least year by year, existence, even though the topics of these documents are often far removed from the concerns of the laity, and their style and tone make them generally illegible to the majority of the faithful. The problem is that this guidance shows a high degree of subjectivity, if not of arbitrariness, insofar as it exposes the faithful to the idiosyncrasies of successive popes, who are themselves influenced by their nationality, their culture, their family, their general education, their religious and theological training, their affective development, their knwoledge or ignorance of scientific, psychological, and sociological insights that are valued in society, their experience of life, their ministry as priests and bishops. The people are at the mercy of a pope's at times questionable interpretations of historical facts, as was the case with Leo XIII and the condemnation of Anglican ordinations. Likewise, they are affected by a pope's theology, by his understanding of the natural law and of the Catholic tradition, as for instance regarding the alleged complementarity of men and women, the purposes of matrimony, the acceptable methods of birth control, or the possibility of the ordination of women. What should, in theory, be a theonomous authority because of its reference to Christ, tends spontaneously to become autonomous, simply because it is wielded by sinful, even if holy, men. To the extent that it is autonomous, it becomes heteronomous for those who are subject to it. If a papal position seems erroneous, Catholics are usually not excessively concerned, for they feel confident that it will change in future years. In the meantime, however, there are always some who are not satisfied with just waiting for another pope.

The very independence of papal authority, gained through centuries of struggle between the temporal and the spiritual swords of Christendom, turned out in the sixteenth century to be the main occasion for criticism of papal authority. Here as elsewhere, every system sews the seeds of its own demise. The claim to supreme authority in interpreting Scripture and tradition invites contradiction, for the obvious reason that the bishop of Rome's authority is itself subordinate to Christ. Being ruled by the scriptural source and the traditional expressions of Christian knowledge, it is open to question by all who have access to this knowledge. As it was formulated at the end of the nineteenth century, the position of the bishop of Rome as successor of Peter sits on a thin line between the one and the many, the one gospel of Christ shared by all the baptized, and the many ways in which this gospel has been and will be perceived and experienced over the centuries.

In this chapter I have looked at principles and problems of ecclesiology, and I have focused attention on a question that is fundamental to the understanding of creation: How can unity and plurality, the one and the many, co-exist? In so doing I have taken the risk of sounding excessively negative before the likelihood of a reconciliation of the Churches. I am truly seeking, however, for the possibility of this reconciliation on the basis of an ecumenical ecclesiology. The next chapter will point to positive elements in the present situation.

CHAPTER 7

PROGRESS AND MODELS

The search for an ecumenical ecclesiology has made considerable progress with several recent advances in ecumenical dialogue that have ecclesiological implications. If the traditions of Lutheranism, Anglicanism, and Catholicism are to become one, we have to start imagining what such a unity could possibly be like. Each in its own way, Lutheranism and Catholicism have had clear views of Christian unity. For the Confession of Augsburg, art. VII, *satis est*, "it is enough," for a community to be a true Church of Christ, that in it the Word be preached and the sacraments be properly administered. For then the Church is subject to the gospel, and the ultimate standard, for the Church as for theology, is the good news, justification by faith, which is God's gift in Jesus Christ. Lutherans therefore should in principle have no problem being one, or becoming one, with any community where it is manifest that faith reigns and that the whole life of the community is ruled by the twofold standard of Word and sacraments.

Counterreformation Catholicism was equally clear: The unity of the Church requires, not only the profession of orthodox faith in keeping with the teaching of the great councils, including the council of Trent, but also communion with the bishop of Rome as a visible sign and instrument of universal unity. In this the dominant accent was placed on the visible marks of the Church as a social institution. It was assumed that this visible Church is precisely the House of God, in which the faithful and the hierarchy are both ruled by the revelation given in Christ, seen as a "deposit of faith" that is to be integrally transmitted. It follows that a dialogue between Lutherans and Catholics ought be focused on the relations between the spiritual and the visible aspects of the Church.

As to Anglicanism, it has always remained somewhat vague, not on the heart of the Church, but on its limits. The Thirty-nine Articles defined the Church in terms that were inspired by the Augsburg Confession: "The visible Church of Christ is a congregation of faithful men in the which the pure Word of God is preached, and the Sacraments be duly administered according to Christ's ordinance, in all those things that of necessity are requisite to the same" (art. XIX). At the same time, however, art. XXXVI maintained the traditional ordination of bishops and ministers, and thus preserved the hierarchic structure of the Church. Anglicans, however, have not lacked imagination in searching for a new organic unity of the Christian Churches, as when Anglican dioceses have been incorporated in United Churches, a process that began with the formation of the Church of South India in 1948. This has not been done without discrimination, for Anglicans have not been part of all schemes of reunion; they did not join the United Church of Canada or the Uniting Church of Australia.

More recently, the idea that reunion should come slowly, through a gradual process of steps and stages, has found fairly general support. The Anglican/Roman Catholic Preparatory Commission envisaged an approach to union by stages, which was suggested by Bishop Christopher Butler. ARCIC-I proceeded to clear the ground by studying the major points of historical divergence between the Catholicism and Anglicanism. If new difficulties have emerged since then between the two Communions, it is largely because other recommendations of the Preparatory Commission have been ignored. "We should cooperate," the Commission wrote in the *Malta Report*, "and not take unilateral action, in any significant changes[1]..." The Commission was thinking of relatively minor changes "in the seasons and major holidays of the Christian Year." If it is valid for small points, however, the principle of cooperation should evidently apply to more substantial changes. When, however, the Episcopal Church, eventually followed by practically the whole Anglican Communion, decided to authorize the ordination of women, this was an unexpected and entirely unilateral action. Whatever one may think of the ultimate necessity or wisdom of this decision, it set aside the process of unity by stages on the basis of mutual cooperation.

Such a process has nonetheless been at work between Anglicans and Lutherans. Intercommunion between them has been adopted as a forward step toward unity that does not require the creation of new ecclesial entities. The process can be observed in the Porvoo plan for communion between the Anglican Churches of the British Isles and

1. *Malta Report*, n.13 (Alan Clark and Colin Davey, *The Work of the Preparatory Commission*, London: Oxford University Press, 1974, p.110). .

the Lutheran Churches of Scandinavia and the Baltic States, that was proposed in October 1992 at Järvenpää, Finland, and was implemented in 1995. Likewise, the Concordat of Agreement between the ELCA and the Episcopal Church, proposed in 1991, was the fruit of a similar hope of growing together through gradual stages.

The international dialogue between Catholics and Lutherans surveyed possible "models of union" in its statement, *Facing Unity* (1980), namely, Organic union, Corporate union, Church Fellowship through Agreement, Conciliar fellowship, Reconciled Diversity, the Union of Florence. It also described possible "forms and phases" of fellowship between Catholics and Lutherans: mutual recognition on the basis of community of faith and community in the sacraments, community of service, including the service of episcopè or government, thus foreseeing a way that would be similar to what had been advocated by the Preparatory Commission between the Catholic and the Anglican Communions. The dialogue was clearly suggesting that the two traditions purposely engage in such a progressive strengthening of pastoral, intellectual, and doctrinal ties as would lead to the point where reunion could not be reasonably delayed.

It was in the spirit of *Facing Unity* that Karl Rahner and Heinrich Fries wrote their book of 1983, *Unity of the Churches, an Actual Possibility*[2]. Through eight theses they proposed that communion be founded on a consensus that would include, (I and II) the fundamental truths expressed in Scripture, the Apostles' and the Nicene creed, as the only dogmas binding on the uniting Churches, (III) the continuation and integrity of "regional partner Churches," corresponding to current denominations, (IVa) acknowledgment of "the meaning and right of the Petrine service of the bishop of Rome," (IVb) respect for the continuing "independence of the partner Churches," (V) the episcopal structure of the hierarchy, (VI) partnership in sharing past histories, (VII) ordination by laying on of hands, (VIII) mutual communion, also called, pulpit and altar fellowship. Such a communion would allow for further growth toward closer unity. The cooperation that would be required for the proposed agendas to turn into a common project has so far failed to provoke wide enthusiasm. The proposals have been mostly ignored. Yet a process has begun that may be called the purification of memory. In fact, the purification of memory is at work at this time among many Churches. The best known instance is the declaration of 7 December

2. New York: Paulist Press, 1985.

1965 by pope Paul VI and patriarch Athenagoras, when "the Churches of Rome and Constantinople lifted the anathemas which had existed between them[3]." By lifting the anathemas they abolished their mutual excommunications, namely the excommunication of patriarch Michael Cerullarios by the legate of Leon IX, Cardinal Humbert de Silva Candida (Humbert de Moyenmoutier when he was a monk in Lorraine) pronounced in 1054. The actual wording of the declaration says that the excommunications are "thrown into oblivion and taken away from the midst of the Church." As he commented on what had just taken place, Paul VI alluded to "the art of forgetting." At a commemorative event ten years later, Metropolitan Meliton, who represented Patriarch Dimitrios II, spoke of now celebrating "an act of memory: memory of the forgetting of the past. Not all the past, but a particular part of the past which must remain the past and only the past." The exact wording of the joint declaration of 1965 was the following:

> Pope Paul VI and Patriarch Athenagoras I in his synod... declare with one accord, a) that they regret the offensive words, the groundless reproaches and the reprovable gestures which on both sides marked the sad events of that period; b) that they equally regret and they remove from the memory and the midst of the Church the sentences of excommunication that followed, the remembrance of which works, up to our own days, as an obstacle to our rapprochement in charity, and that they commit them to oblivion; c) that they finally deplore the unfortunate precedents and the later events which... finally led to an effective break of ecclesial communion[4].

This wording is of great importance in the search for ways of reconciliation. It includes the following elements: 1) The damage done in the past by a Church or its leaders to another Church must be truly regretted. 2) It should be voluntarily and mutually committed to oblivion, which requires a great deal of mutual reflection and spiritual preparation. 3) Only on these two conditions, when it has been "lifted" from the midst of the Church, can it lose its continuing divisive power.

---

3. *Information Service. The Secretariat for Promoting Christian Unity*, n.31, 1976/II, p.1.

4. Text in *La Documentation catholique*, 2 January 1976, p.67.

❦

Tradition, the handing down of doctrine and customs from one age to the next, has functioned in Christian history as the memory of the Church. Nothing can be transmitted unless it has been remembered, and nothing can be remembered unless it has been either received from the past or experienced in the life of those who pass it on. In so far as the Church is guided by the Holy Spirit, the process of tradition is protected and guided. The heart of what is transmitted is of course the gospel. Yet in all Churches many things have been transmitted along with the gospel, such as, liturgical rituals, practices of piety, principles of theology, linguistic conventions, Christian writings, artistic achievements, forms of imagination and art, customs and familiar ways of action, and also, further removed from the heart of the gospel, political opinions, social conventions, sexual stereotypes, cultural assumptions, one-sided options for a class or a caste over another, tribal or national identifications, superstitious beliefs and practices. Whether it is defined in the singular as "the very life of the Church," or in the collective plural as the sum total of whatever Christian generations have passed on to one another, the tradition has never been pure. Like the Church itself it always stands in need of purification.

The means of the purification of tradition is the practice of hope. For hope is closely connected with memory, as one may learn from the analysis of union with God in Book III of John of the Cross's *Ascent of Mount Caramel*. The subtitle of this book in the standard American translation says: "This book treats of purgation in the active night of memory and the will. It presents doctrine about the attitude required in the apprehensions of these two faculties so that a soul may reach union with God in perfect hope and charity[5]." It was the profound insight of John of the Cross that the purification, which is needed before any creature can see God, includes the purification of memory. What then should be remembered of the many experiences that have occurred in the pilgrimage of life? Because it is radically turned to the future, hope can survive only if memory has been cleansed of the unhealthy traces of the past. In this sense memory is the faculty of forgetting what is no longer needed, in order to be free for the grace that is coming from the Spirit. Only those who have been disencumbered of their own weight can jump ahead blindly into the love of God. Thus memory is the faculty

5. *The Collected Works of St. John of the Cross*, Washington, DC.: ICS Publications, p. 267.

of remembering because it is first of all the faculty of forgetting what is not worth remembering. What is actually remembered is shrouded in a cloud of unknowing, without which the mind would be unable to function, cluttered as it would be by images of every past action, every minute lived, every deed done, every thought thought, every word heard, every word pronounced, every sunset seen, every storm weathered. The insight of John of the Cross has been abundantly confirmed by psychoanalysis: In order to act in the present and in view of the future one needs to be freed from the weight of past thoughts and actions.

Memory and Hope was the title of a volume by Dietrich Ritschl, which did not receive the attention it deserved because it came out shortly after the English version of Jürgen Moltmann's *Theology of Hope*[6]. Both books were focused on the notion that hopes lies at the heart of the Church. The Christian hope is primarily oriented toward the fulfillment of the divine promises in the eschaton, and secondarily on tentative approaches to the Kingdom of God, which are dreamed of and partially outlined in the Church. The singular merit of Ritschl was that he centered his study on the sense of the ongoing presence of Christ that has always been very much alive among the faithful. The Church is the realm in which the Christian believers experience *Christus praesens*.

Reading the patristic doctrines in light of this fundamental principle, Ritschl was led to favor the Greek over the Latin tradition, namely, the uplifting sense of participating by grace, today, in the coming Kingdom of God through the gift of the Spirit, in what may be called an iconic horizon, rather than the moral yet down- dragging sense of having to struggle with the human condition of original sin and actual sins, and in this dire state to hope for actual graces that may keep the faithful in the sanctifying grace received in baptism. As a community embracing the whole world in its concerns, the Church needs to be disencumbered from things remembered that ought to be forgotten. The motor of its ongoing life and of its continuity through the centuries is precisely a spiritual instinct by which the community sorts out what needs to be preserved for the next generation of the baptized and what should be relinquished or, if not actually forgotten, at least committed to oblivion. Such an overcoming of the past can only be done in the light of the

---

6. Jürgen Moltmann, *Theology of Hope: On the Ground and Implications of a Christian Eschatology*, New York: Harper and Row, 1967; Dietrich Ristchl, *Memory and Hope. An Inquiry concerning the Presence of Christ*, New York: Macmillan, 1975.

future, in expectation of the eschaton as the faithful get nearer to it, slowly, day after day, year after year, century after century, millennium after millennium.

The expectation of the eschaton is the ultimate Christian hope, as is implied by the words which close the New Testament, "Amen. Come, Lord Jesus" (Apoc. 22,20). Whether the break of their unity took place in the fifth, the eleventh, or the sixteenth century, the Churches have sought for strength and stability in remembering the why and wherefore of their original separation. Having become part of their cherished patrimony, this remembering has nurtured the permanence of their separations. The obverse movement, toward reconciliation, requires the opposite attitude: to be detached from oneself, from one's idiosyncrasies and private characteristics, from one's history, so that one may be free to embrace the others, to cherish the talents of each, and to own the history of all. This is the ultimate meaning of loving the neighbor as oneself. It is true catholicity: to welcome the criticism of us that comes from estranged brothers and sisters, so that the rancors that preceded and have followed the past breaks of communion may be truly exorcised. It is the meaning of "lifting of the excommunications" between Rome and Constantinople.

❧

The prophetic gesture of Paul VI and Athenagoras I was followed by an analogous gesture in the very different context of Lutheran/Catholic relations, when, on October 31, 1999, the two sides officially declared obsolete the condemnations inherited from the sixteenth century in the matter of justification. The declaration adopted by the two sides does not imply that either side blames its ancestors for doing what they felt in conscience bound to do. It is a recognition that the condemnations were based in part on misunderstanding of the teaching of the opponent, and that the and aggressiveness with which each side looked at the other at the time has become obsolete and dysfunctional.

Unlike the statement of Paul VI and patriarch Athenagoras on the excommunications of 1054, the wording of the Declaration does not suggest oblivion. Given the common focus of Lutheranism and of Catholicism on the formulation of doctrine, it is a brief specification of the correct meaning of the doctrines involved. As befits a coming of minds of Lutherans and Catholics, both of whom have entertained an Augustinian theology of sin, it also implies on each side acknowledgment of shortcomings, awareness of sin, repentance, renunciation to self-achievements, reliance on Christ alone through faith alone. One cannot abolish the past, and if past misdeeds or errors are committed to oblivion they are not thereby forgotten. They simply become the occasion of remembering the event of their oblivion. One may well ask, how far can the Churches go in renouncing their past without losing their identity?

In a sense, loss of identity at a superficial level can only be beneficial to the discovery or recovery of identity at a deeper or higher level. *Wo Es war, soll Ich werden* ("Where there was It, there should be I"), Sigmund Freud wrote as the concluding sentence of *The Psychopathology of Everyday Life* (1901). Where we were "It," a non-thinking entity that simply existed by virtue of a momentum passively received from the past, an authentic "I" should emerge, regretting the past while taking responsibility for it, personalizing and liberating the present, and pouring energy into building a reconciling future.

The expression, sister-Churches, has been customary, in Roman official language, to designate the Orthodox Churches. Paul VI used it also in reference to the Anglican Communion, but he saw this sisterhood in the future, as a goal to be aimed at or a model of the communion that needs to be restored:

> There will be no seeking to lessen the legitimate prestige and the worthy patrimony of piety and usage proper to the Anglican Church when the Roman Catholic Church—this humble "Servant of the servants of God"—is able to embrace her ever beloved sister in the one authentic communion of the family of Christ: a communion of origin and of faith, a communion of priesthood and of rule, a communion of the saints in the freedom of love of the spirit of Jesus[7].

One point needs clarification: Does the "communion of rule" refer to the rule of faith or to the rule of canon law? Without being suspicious of papal intentions one may still ask: How far should the Churches go in their search for sisterhood? The question can be answered with the help of a series of ecumenical dialogues that have received little publicity. These are the dialogues between Chalcedonian and non-Chalcedonian

---

7. Robert Hale, *Canterbury and Rome, Sister Churches*, New York: Paulist Press, 1982, p.16.

Churches. At Vatican II Pope Kyrillos VI of Alexandria sent observers who represented the Coptic Church of Egypt. Following the council a dialogue started between Cairo and Rome. A striking achievement of this dialogue was a doctrinal agreement that was signed on 10 May, 1973, by Paul VI, "Bishop of Rome and Pope of the Catholic Church," and Schenouda III, "Pope of Alexandria and Patriarch of the See of St. Mark." This agreement affirmed a common allegiance to the Council of Nicaea and acknowledged the exemplary leadership of St. Athanasius. In regard to the incarnation, the text stated:

> ...we confess one faith in the One Triune God, the divinity of the Only Begotten Son of God, the Second Person of the Trinity, the Word of God, the effulgence of His glory and the express image of His substance, who for us was incarnate, assuming for Himself a real body with a rational soul, and who shared with us our humanity but without sin. We confess that our Lord and God and Savior and King of us all, Jesus Christ, is perfect God with respect to His Divinity, perfect man with respect to His humanity. In Him His divinity is united to His humanity in a real, perfect union without mingling, without commiction, without confusion, without alteration, without division, without separation. His divinity did not separate from His humanity for an instant, not for the twinkling of an eye. He who is eternal and invisible became visible in the flesh, and took upon Himself the form of a servant. In Him are preserved all the properties of the divinity and all the properties of the humanity, together in a real, perfect, indivisible and inseparable union[8].

The Coptic Church of Egypt, as also Churches in Ethiopia, Syria, and Armenia, severed their links with both Rome and Constantinople when they denied the ecumenicity and rejected the teaching of the council of Chalcedon (451). This fourth ecumenical council, however, duly recognized in the Byzantine and the Western traditions, played a major role in shaping the religious conscience of the West. Following the lead of Pope Leo I, Chalcedon endorsed the doctrine contained in his letter to the council, the so-called Tome of Leo. The pope's intent was to steer a middle course between Nestorius of Constantinople and Eutyches of Alexandria. Hence the deliberate emphasis of the council of Chalcedon on the distinction of the divine and human natures in

---

8. *Information Service. Pontifical Council for Promoting Christian Unity*, n. 76, 1991 (1), p.9.

the incarnate Word, and on the unity of divinity and humanity in the divine Person of the Word Incarnate. The agreement of 1973, however, implies that it is possible to profess the orthodox faith without endorsing the Christological formula of Chalcedon. In other words, Paul VI admitted that the true faith has been preserved, in the Coptic Church of Egypt, by those who denied the validity of the fourth ecumenical council. Regardless of the Chalcedonian formula, the creed of Nicaea is therefore sufficient for orthodoxy, as long as it is properly interpreted in the context of the traditional liturgies.

Since 1973 similar statements have involved the other Churches that used to be called, Monophysite. This term, used historically, refers to the interpretation of the formulas of St. Cyril of Alexandria by Eutyches, not to the use of the same formulas that has been received in the non-Chalcedonian Churches at least since Severus of Antioch, in the second half of the fifth century. Analogous statements have been made with the Assyrian Church of Iraqn which does not even recognize the council of Ephesus (431), and rejects the condemnation of Nestorius. Whatever Nestorius taught (and recent scholarship tends to clear him of formal heresy) about the harmony of the divine and the human in Christ, the Assyrian Church is now seen as escaping the condemnation of the Council of Ephesus.

These agreements imply a far-reaching and somewhat surprising principle: Orthodoxy of faith is not identical with its formulation[9]. In the case of the Coptic Church, they mean that the once contentious formula of St. Cyril of Alexandria, *mia physis tou Theou Logou sesarkomene* ("one incarnate nature of the divine Logos"), as it is understood in the Ancient Oriental Churches, expresses the true faith, in spite of the Chalcedonian affirmation of two natures (*physeis*) "in one person and one substance" (*eis en prosopon kai mian hypostasin*). The two natures of the incarnate Lord constitute one reality, not two. In other words, the idiosyncratic formulations of one party, even when endorsed by a council that is regarded as ecumenical, need not be a condition of union. The proper condition of union is that the formulae of the two sides be regarded, if not as identical, at least as complementary or equivalent. In order to reach this point, the two sides have to recognize the traditional

---

9. This may be related to what John XXIII said in his address at the first session of Vatican Council II: "The substance of the ancient doctrine of the deposit of faith is one thing, and the way in which it is presented is another."

formulations of each as legitimate, even where their languages diverge to the point of verbal contradiction.

The process at work in these dialogues is precisely a cure of rejuvenation. Past condemnations are regretted and committed to oblivion. The time of harmony before the condemnations is brought to mind and remembered. The Churches implicitly return to their unity before the estrangement that separated them, and they do so, no longer in the naïveté of their former innocence, but with the scars of their historical estrangement. They recover something that was lost in their isolation, and that needs their mutual harmony to survive. Cleaning the memory of the antagonistic traces of condemnations entails the bringing back of past moments that were forgotten, moments when the accepted formulas of faith were not so exclusive as they later became, when they were closer to the original simplicity of the Gospel and had not yet hardened into tests of correct belief.

It was a similar nostalgia for the youth of the Church that lay behind Martin Luther's insistence on Scripture alone. If the Church's memory strives to go back to the first moment of the faith, what it finds is nothing more, though nothing less, than the Scriptures. Here one reaches a far-reaching principle that should be at work in ecumenical dialogues, especially between Protestants and Catholics. It may hold the key to future reconciliations. The principle of *scriptura sola*, however, which was held in some form by the great scholastics of the thirteenth century, is not, as such, restrictive of appeals to the Fathers, to the councils, and to the consensus of theologians, for all of these too should witness to the truth of the Scriptures. The principle was misread in the anti-Lutheran polemics of the sixteenth century, as it also was eventually misread by many Protestants. Yet it was intended, and it ought to function, as a fountain of youth, a return to the youth of the Church. At the end of the second century St. Irenaeus called the faith a *depositum juvenescens*, a received deposit that has the effect of rejuvenating the receiver. It is received in the Scriptures, and it renovates the Church's life as the Scriptures are read and explained by Fathers and councils in the tradition that transmits them faithfully. How far along these lines the Holy See at the present time would be prepared to go in reassessing the parting of ways of the sixteenth century I do not know. Yet one cannot set a priori limits to the rejuvenation of the Church.

❦

In 1990 I published a book on a question on which I wish now to reflect briefly[10]. Undoubtedly, the declaration that Anglican Ordinations have no effect, that was made by pope Leo XIII in 1896 in the apostolic letter *Apostolicae curae*, is a sore that stands in dire need of healing. When Leo XIII's chief adviser on the matter, the Master of the Sacred Palace, Rafaele Pierotti, presented his recommendation on 28 May 1896, he held that a "new, solemn, formal, and explicit" condemnation of Anglican Orders, based on defect of form and defect of intention intention in the Ordinal, was necessary and opportune. Having listened to the future cardinal Merry del Val, who represented the archbishop of Westminster in Rome, he and Pope Leo naïvely believed that such a condemnation would impel a great number of high-Church Anglicans to seek refuge in the Catholic Church, as John Henry Newman, for other reasons than doubt about ordination, had done in 1845. No such movement, however, took place. Since the Vatican archives for that period have been opened, we now know, not only that half the members of the Commission on Anglican Ordinations set up by Leo XIII favored recognition of their validity, but also that the Commission was disbanded by the pope before it could reach a consensus. Moreover, Catholic theologians who do not follow the neoscholastic theology of Leo XIII can easily detect basic weaknesses in the reasoning of *Apostolicae curae*. If a reconciliation of memories is sought between Anglicans and Catholics, it has to pass through a revision of Leo's judgment on Anglican Orders.

Pope Paul VI was certainly not mistaken in 1975, when he wrote to Archbishop Coggan that the ordination of women in the Anglican Communion would be a "grave obstacle" on the way to unity[11]. In canon law the problem is quite simple. If one word was changed in canon 1024 (*vir* to *homo*), the ordination of women would be authorized. The theological question, however, is more involved than this would indicate. The Latin word, *vir*, has been in the canons that regulate ordination since at least the Decree of Gratian (1150/51). On the basis of the canons most of the scholastics held that the ordination of a woman is impossible. They generally justified this impossibility by reference to the natural subordination of women to men in the philosophical and politi-

---

10. *A Review of Anglican Order. The Problem and the Solution*, Collegeville, MN: Liturgical Press, 1990.

11. Letter, 30 November 1975.

cal traditions that they knew. The major exception was the Franciscan John Duns Scotus, who believed that the Church could not possibly be guilty of such an enormous injustice to half of humanity. Impressed as he was by the constancy of the tradition, however, he assumed that the decision, the fundamental reasons for which remain unknown, must be attributed to Jesus Christ, whom no one may judge![12]

Nonetheless, women were certainly ordained to the diaconate in the East in patristic times. And it has always been held that the diaconate, the presbyterate, and the episcopate, constitute only one sacrament. If women at one time did receive one degree of the sacrament, it is difficult to see why they could not receive the totality of the sacrament when the situation is ripe for it. The problem, however, is now further complicated, on the one hand, by John Paul II's puzzling statement that the Church is not "authorized" to ordain women[13], and, on the other, by the fact that, in the circumstances of Communist persecution, two Catholic bishops in Czechoslovakia did ordain several women to the priesthood[14]. More recently, the suggestion made by the Roman Congregation for the Doctrine of the Faith, that the non-ordainability of women is assured by the general infallibility of bishops in their ordinary magisterium, has deepened the confusion[15], since it contradicts the stipulation of canon 749 §3, that no doctrine has been defined infallibly unless this is clearly manifest.

This point may not be of immediate interest to Lutherans. Yet insofar as the differing Christian traditions are groping for a new form of organic

12. See my essay, "The Roman Catholic Church," in Michael P. Hamilton and Nancy S. Montgomery, eds., *The Ordination of Women: pro and con*, New York: Morehouse-Barlow, 1975, p.112-125.

13. Address to German bishops in their visit *ad limina*, 30 November 1999. On the one hand, in the absence of traditional criteria for what the Church is authorized to do, it is impossible to know what this is until the Church actually does it. On the other hand, the Church over the ages has done various things it certainly was not authorized to do, like handing over prisoners of the Inquisition to the secular power so that they would be burnt alive.

14. Miriam Therese Winter, *Out of the Depths. The Story of Ludmilla Javorova, Ordained Roman Catholic Priest*, New York: Crossroad, 2001.

15. Note on the "motu proprio" *Ad tuendam fidem*; the note is signed by Cardinal Joseph Ratzinger and Msgr Tarcisio Bertone.

unity, all should wish the best for each. The moves I have considered could have an effect of rejuvenation that would take the Churches, not back to their former harmony in a time that is gone, but forward toward growing together into unity of faith and communion. Such an access to new youth would not erase the Reformation. It would help to remember it in a new light, as an opportunity for growth that was not handled equally well in all the Churches, but that has never been unfruitful.

CHAPTER 8

PROBLEMS OF RECEPTION[1]

After the general excitement of novelty and the arduous work done during the council, one had to face the task of reception and application. In terms of structures, this meant forming post-conciliar commissions, organizing the national conferences of bishops, creating an international advisory body of theologians, instituting the Synod of Bishops, updating the code of law. The post-conciliar commission for liturgical reform was the best known, because it directly affected the life and piety of the People of God. But others were just as important.

These commissions had to follow a wavering line between two extremes, for there soon emerged two contradictory movements. At one extreme, a chaotic experimentation soon treated as obsolete the principles of Vatican II for reform and doctrine. At the other extreme, the anti-conciliar revolt of a few questioned the validity of the Vatican Council II. Clergy and people found themselves pulled in opposite directions by these departures from the balance that had been reached in 1962-1965. Begun in several places as a protest against liturgy in the vernacular, the reaction found its leader in a retired missionary archbishop, Marcel Lefebvre (1905-1991), who denied the right of Paul VI to alter the liturgical ritual that had been promulgated by Pius V in 1570 "in perpetuity[2]."

In these conditions the Catholic hierarchy, following Paul VI, wished to steer a middle course. This consisted mainly in adopting and maintaining two stances. Firstly, the explicit decisions of the council were applied, though with moderate speed. The liturgical reform was gradual, decreed piece by piece through a series of changes, the succession of which was

---

1. Decree *Pro primum*, 14 July, 1570.

2. I happened to be at the residence of a bishop in South Africa, sitting in a lounge with the bishop and several of his priests. The radio was turned for the latest news. When the word came about *Humanae vitae* the bishop jumped from his armchair and exclaimed: "He has lost his mind! He is mad!" We spent the next two hours trying to draft a short statement on birth control.

a partial cause of confusion. Yet it was also brutal, in that the liturgy of Pius V, which survived partially in the first of the officially authorized canons, was outlawed in its original form, rather than left open as a temporary option. Secondly, the drawing of further conclusions from what had been explicitly stated by the council was definitely discouraged. The result was a Janus-like position that was not likely to satisfy many of those for whom the council had been an exciting experience of discovery. The prudential position of the post-conciliar commissions entailed a fear of the extremes that was far removed from the serenity and joy of the conciliar experience. The post-conciliar Church found itself caught between the two horns of regressive interpretation and liberal progressivism, or, to borrow the secular language of 1968, between gauchist deviation and reactionary conservatism. The reasons for this, it seems to me, are of three kinds. First, there was a glaring lacuna at Vatican II itself. Second, there were hesitancies on the part of Paul VI. Third, there was the heavy weight of institutional inertia.

Very little thought was given at Vatican II to the follow-up of the council. The mind of most of those who contributed to updating the Church still generally functioned in the mindset of the nineteenth century, when the theological revival of the Restoration filled the gap that had been left by the destruction of the universities in the French Revolution. After the experiments of "traditionalism" in France and Italy, and the rise of the school of Tübingen in Germany, theology settled in the ultramontanist mode of Pius IX and Vatican Council I. Later on it adopted the neo-scholastic framework that Leo XIII promoted. The more progressive thought of Cardinal Newman was generally ignored, and the insights of the Modernists were savagely hunted down under Pius X. By and large the neo-scholastic paradigm had not changed in the 1960's, outside of some distinguished theological circles in French- and German-speaking lands. Many of the bishops who arrived in Rome for the beginning of Vatican II, including, it would seem, the majority of the Americans, expected pope John to tell them what he wanted. They would vote for it. And the council would be over in a few weeks' time.

This anticipation followed the natural bent of the ultramontane mentality. Pius IX had indeed consulted the bishops of the world before defining the immaculate conception of Mary, and so had Pius XII before defining the assumption. In both cases, however, the pope's desire was well known, and it was not surprising that the result of the consultation overwhelmingly concurred with his desire. Bishops in general were not used to assuming responsibility for the whole Church. They left this concern to the bishop of Rome, and they willingly gave him their support when he needed it. This, however, was not what John XXIII or Paul VI had in mind. Nor was it what a number of European bishops and cardinals wished for.

The ultramontane turn of mind was rejected in the early days of the council, when bishops criticized the agenda prepared by the Roman curia, and the council searched for its own way. The lingering ultramontane mentality, however, was not so easily discarded. The fundamental problem was due to too wide a gap between the passivity before Roman decisions to which the Church had grown used to, and the initiatives that had become urgent. Because papal wishes had, over the years, obtained force of law and Roman decisions were unquestioningly applied, most bishops did not foresee that the council required a different process of reception.

Reception as a theological question concerns the process by which previous data—from Scripture, from early or later tradition, from anterior practice—are received as authoritative in subsequent ages. Research about this process is related to current reflection about communion (koinonia) as a central category of ecclesiology. The Church is a communion, of humans with God, of humans among themselves. Communion can be analyzed at the philosophical, social, and political levels, since there cannot be a meaningful coexistence of many in one society without a degree of mutual participation in one another's values and concerns. As the world is growing into a global village, learning about one another has become a necessity for collectivities as for people. Reciprocal relations between cultures are a requirement of the one world that is undoubtedly in the making. Mutual participation is the central piece in this unification of humankind. In this context, meaningful coexistence means a coexistence that is not only factual, as when hostile nations happen to be neighbors. Coexistence must become creative, so that opportunities may emerge for an increased progress in true civilization, that is, in the spiritual process by which humanity becomes more sisterly and fraternal.

To this growing together the Christian experience adds the possibility of a higher level of communion. As they realize that their existence is truly in Christ, the faithful have access to a higher degree of their humanity. In line with the biblical tradition that they share with Jews they are aware of the image of God in themselves. Beyond the Old Testament, however, they also participate by faith in the eternal filiation of Jesus Christ, thus sharing the gift of the Trinitarian life of God, the Father, the Son, and the Spirit. This is ecclesial communion, which is ultimately identical with the spiritual dimension of the Church.

The reception of doctrine creates communion between the past and the present. What was decided in the remote or recent past is accepted and becomes normative in the present. The form of ecclesial communion that obtains at any moment has thus been partly determined by the Church's past experience. If the Church has a hierarchy, it is because the leadership of the apostles' successors in the early centuries was received as normative by subsequent ages. The ecumenical situation illustrates the same point. The ecumenical hope is that the Churches will be able to restore communion with one another. This, however, cannot be done until all Churches accept as their own, not only each one's linear past, but also that of other Churches, which they may have rejected formerly.

Thus reception is a constitutive element of tradition understood as the complex movement trough which the experience of past ages is passed on from one generation to the next. It implies two moments: passing on, giving, teaching, *ecclesia docens* (the teaching Church), and hearing, receiving, accepting, *ecclesia discens* (the learning Church). *Docens* and *discens*, teaching and learning, are not coterminous with hierarchy and laity, but with the past and the present. Such a tradition implies conciliarity, for the Church functions in conciliar fashion when it acknowledges and receives its past. In this sense the whole Church attended Vatican II, bishops acting in the name of their local Churches, superiors general in the name of their communities, theologians in the name of the academe and of the theological schools that contribute to Catholic scholarship, lay observers and journalists in the name of the People of God and of the broader public opinion, ecumenical observers in the name of the communities that sent them. This process of tradition and reception is both geographic and temporal. The passing on is done by the Church represented and gathered in particular locations, and the receiving is done by the Church at large, spread out over the world.

If this is the reality of reception, then understanding is an integral part of it. One can of course apply instructions that one does not understand. This is commonly done in modern technology. People drive cars without knowing how the motor works. They use computers without understanding how their hardware and software function. Indeed, modern technology has so mushroomed that it is impossible for one person to learn the details of all the machines that one commonly uses. The case, however, is different with spiritual realities. The very nature of faith and its practice demand that the whole person be engaged. The faithful ought to believe, in the phrase of St. Anselm, "in order to understand" (*credo ut intelligam*). Faith is blind, a darkness, a night, in that it rests on total trust in the revelation given in Christ, knowing that the fact of revelation cannot be established on empirical evidence, and that the content of what is revealed is by no means self-evident. The many attempts that have been made to build rational systems of Christian apologetics witness to this aspect of the experience of faith, for they all fail to carry out their promise. Faith is not the daughter of rationality.

Once it has taken hold of the heart and mind, however, faith becomes a light that changes night into day. In its full unfolding it so impacts the mind that it gives rise to new insights into reality and to new thought processes. In this, faith is similar to supernatural charity, when one gives of oneself beyond what is possible to merely natural love. It is also similar to theological hope, which discerns the ultimate designs of God beyond what is seen, touched, and felt in the current experience of life. Admittedly, this discernment is never total, never fully achieved. Neither faith nor love or hope is ever perfect in the disciples of Jesus. Rather, faith is an ongoing movement that goes both forward and within. As Gregory of Nyssa described it in his *Life of Moses*, on the model of the Hebrews' march toward Mount Sinai, the search for Christian perfection is a long pilgrimage. Moses himself never entered the Holy Land, but only saw it from a distance. Likewise, if the understanding of faith may trace the lineaments of the mystery that has been revealed, it never reaches full knowledge in the present life, for then faith itself would become superfluous, replaced by the vision of God.

These remarks on the understanding of faith are relevant to the way the council's reforms and orientations affect the life of faith, love, and hope in the Catholic community. The council cannot be truly received, applied, and lived where it is not at least partly understood. A true understanding of the council, however limited, brings a new focus to Christian living, a shift of attention, a change of horizon from what was before. It requires willingness to look for a new focus, to shift the beam of one's attention, to travel toward a new horizon.

The post-conciliar developments could have been foreseen. Indeed, some of the conciliar commissions actively prepared the post-conciliar period during the council itself. This was notably the case with the Secretariat for Christian Unity, which gave a great deal of thought to the future directory of ecumenism even before the decree *Unitatis redintegratio* was composed, debated, and adopted.

Another set of data was bound to affect the reception of the council. I will not speculate, as has been done, on the character of Paul VI, that some journalists have called Hamlet-like. Whatever the orientations of his own psyche, Paul VI was a great pope, but even a great pope can make tactical mistakes.

The chief of these came from the decision that certain questions should not be discussed in the council, and should be reserved to himself. Such was the question of birth control. After several bishops raised the problem Pope Paul made it clear that it was not on the conciliar agenda, and that he intended to study the matter and to issue a statement in due time. The question was *sub studio*, "under study." Pope Paul's eventual answer to the question came in the encyclical *Humanae vitae*. It caused an unexpected turmoil in the Summer of 1967. To arrive at his conclusion, the pope had created an advisory commission, which was not able to follow the consensus principle of Vatican II. Like numerous committees in contemporary politics and business, it proceeded on majority rule, the minority composing a dissenting report. In the context of the Church, however, such a practice is confusing. At Vatican I, the sizable minority that opposed the definition of papal infallibility chose to leave the scene rather than break the principle of unanimity by issuing a position paper of its own. At Vatican II small minorities voted against the documents, but they did not publish dissenting statements, with the belated exception of Marcel Lefebvre.

The advisory commission having operated in a non-conciliar manner, one cannot entirely blame Pope Paul for not being satisfied with its findings. He set the reports aside, and, after a long enough a time to let false rumors form and spread, reached and published his own conclusion, which was not fully identical with either position, majority or minority, in the advisory Commission. It was in any case contrary to what a sizable portion of the Catholic community hoped for, including a number of bishops and moral theologians[3].

This is not the place to discuss the intrinsic merits or demerits of Pope Paul's theology of marriage. My concern is with the atmosphere that was then created for reception of the council. By its very nature, a council of *aggiornamento* is open to all areas where an updating may be needed. That a review of moral teaching in matters of sexuality was proper is self-evident, given the place of sexuality in Freudian psychoanalysis and in the schools of psychology that have grown out of it, to say nothing of the growing social acceptance of sexual freedom. The blocking of public theological debate on the matter had the dire consequence that theological anthropology remained frozen at the point where neoscholasticism left it. And this point is, I believe, untenable.

After the council, another reserved area concerned the place and functions of women in the Church, and especially the question of the ordination of women. The problem had been confronted in the scholastic discussions of the Middle Ages. It had been touched upon in the collections of canon law, though without any feeling of urgency. There existed no medieval movement regarding of the ordination of women. At the most, there was a distrust of the preaching that women practiced in some marginal sects. Only in the nineteenth century was the question raised in earnest, when the Holiness Churches in America began to ordain women[4]. This initiative had no impact on Catholic thought. In the twentieth century the ordination of women in all but the most conservative Protestant Churches was itself not considered relevant to the Catholic theology of orders: Ministers, it was commonly thought, are not priests in the Catholic sense of the term. The question was nevertheless raised in the context of Catholic Poland. A visionary mystic, Sister Maria Felicia Koslowska (1862-1921), started a movement, later

3. See my article, *The Ordination of Women* (One in Christ, 1987/3, 200-211), originally a paper presented at a meeting of the Faith and Order Commission of New Mexico.

4. I attempted this in *Woman in Christian Tradition*, South Bend: University of Notre Dame Press, 1973.

called Mariavite (from *Mariae vitam imitantes*, "imitating Mary's life"), in which women, on the model of the Virgin Mary, were the dominant leaders. She and her followers were eventually excommunicated. It was not, however, this Polish happening that caused the anguish of Paul VI over the ordination of women. It was rather its eventual authorization in the Anglican Communion, a Church with which Pope Paul, since his days as archbishop of Milan, had been eager to develop close relations. Not surprisingly, Paul VI saw these ordinations as "a new and grave obstacle" to reunion, though he did not make clear whether he regarded them as valid or invalid.

Again, I am not drawing attention primarily to Paul VI's theology of ordination or to his theological anthropology, but to the way he faced the problem. Although Pope Paul did not formally reserve the question to himself, he made it quite clear that, unlike birth control, the ordination of women was not under study. This was equivalently stated in two letters to the archbishop of Canterbury, Donald Coggan (November 30, 1975, responding to the archbishop's letter of July 9, and March 23, 1976, responding to a letter of February 10). The Catholic Church, he stated, holds that the ordination of women cannot be accepted. He mentioned three reasons: the testimony of Scripture on Christ's choice of the apostles; the Church's constant practice; the constant position of the living magisterium that the exclusion of women from the priesthood is in keeping with God's plan for the Church.

The ordination of women touches more than the discipline and theology of sacraments. It brings up fundamental points of Christian anthropology. One cannot discuss the place of women in the Church without considering their place in humanity. Blocking all possibility of a theological development of the sacrament of orders in relation to the ordination of women to the priesthood assumes that Christian anthropology should remain frozen at a scholastic or neoscholastic position concerning the distinction between men and women in the related orders of creation and of grace. All the popes of the twentieth century before and after Vatican II took it for granted that the proper model of female-male relationships is provided by the natural structure of sexual polarity. This polarity has been understood in terms of complementarity. Over the centuries complementary roles in procreation and in the rearing of children have inspired complementarities in social, economic, and political functions. And these in turn have determined the complementarity of men and women in the Church, notably in regard to liturgy and to teaching. However, the translation of the sexual polarity of men and women into social complementarity in all areas of life was itself determined by education, in addition to what may be suggested by nature. As tasks had to be divided in the early human groups, men became hunters and warriors; women became food gatherers and home-keepers. Education in this area has evolved but slightly since the prehistory of humankind.

Taken as a model for relationships between men and women, complementarity has been oppressive of women. This was implicitly recognized when the first chapters of Genesis attributed the domination of women by men to punishment for the fall of Eve. What was needed in the middle 1960's was not a reassertion of the complementarity model, but a search for a new model of relationships[5]. Cautious and understandable as it was, the position of Paul VI resulted in stifling the freshness of theological debate that had been operative during the council. The reception of conciliar decisions was thereby troubled from the start. Reservation of certain areas of doctrine and discipline, now placed out of reach of theological debate, implied that the council was treated as a finished product rather than as the seeding of new growth in the Church's garden.

Boxing up the council's impetus turned out to be deeply harmful. On the one hand, it is in the nature of discourse that the meaning of a text goes beyond the explicit intent of its authors. It belongs to readers to discover the meaning for themselves in their situation. Blocking the unfolding of what may have been implicit in the conciliar texts was not only arbitrary. It was already contrary to what was happening in the post-conciliar commission on the liturgy, and in the liturgy of Paul VI himself, when the use of the vernacular was extended beyond what Vatican II had explicitly stated. In addition, the official blocking of debate took place precisely when those areas of concern were being made extremely sensitive by feminist developments over which the Catholic hierarchy could have no control.

---

5. These "observations" (*Animadversiones*) were sent to the Catholic chair of ARCIC, Bishop Alan Clark, along with a covering letter from Cardinal Ratzinger, on March 27, 1982; they were communicated to the Episcopal Conferences on April 2.

❧

One can readily admit that mistakes made at different levels in the council affected its follow-up and the first stages of its reception. The decision that has touched most people the most was the process chosen for the implementation of liturgical reform. As far as the people in the Church were concerned, this reform required the most adjustment, since by its very nature it touched the life of everyone in every land. Certainly the authorization of official prayer in vernacular languages had been asked for by such a number of people that the idea was by no means new. While no general movement had objected to the principle of a sacred language or of Latin in particular, there had been, since the end of the seventeenth century, a progressive loss of Latin as the basic language of Western Europe. By the middle of the twentieth century Latin was no longer taught in all second-level schools, and many students went through their university studies without knowing a word of Latin. Now, when the Western Church lost the use of Greek in the fifth and sixth centuries it was cut off from easy access to most of the patristic sources of doctrine. Being thus already impoverished in the knowledge of its own tradition it was now being cut off from easy access to its specific Latin heritage. One could regret this phenomenon. Pope John did in his apostolic letter, *Veterum sapientia* (22 February, 1962), the principle of which was obsolete, and the recommendations inapplicable. Latin had become a dead language.

More drastic than the passage to the vernacular were the changes in the ritual of the Eucharist and of some other sacraments. In the six-teenth century the missal of Pius V had barely modified the ritual of the medieval mass. The missal of Paul VI abolished the missal of Pius V, and introduced options between several new canons. Alterations of the Church's common prayer need careful handling, and they should always be prepared and accompanied by an extensive reeducation of clergy and people. This, by and large, was not done. Bishops were taken up by the demands of their dioceses, where important decisions had often been delayed because of the ordinary's long absences during the council. What proportion of the clergy had followed the conciliar debates in depth and were able to explain the reforms to the people, is difficult to establish. It was presumably a small minority. On the whole, the implementation of the liturgical reforms was not satisfactory because of inadequate preparation.

This inadequate preparation was a dimension of institutional inertia, of the reluctance of any administration, whether in business, in politics, or in religion, to learn techniques and methods that would require a drastic overhaul of accustomed practices, and bring about the obsolescence of accustomed administrative rules. It was for this reason that the Roman Curia, after remaining relatively quiescent under Paul VI, sought to regain its power as soon as it could do so. In his cautious reform of the Curia Pope Paul had downgraded the Holy Office, which was no longer the *suprema congregatio* overlooking all other Roman dicasteries. In addition, the council had foreseen a relative autonomy of national episcopal conferences, the active participation of a Synod of Bishops in coresponsibility for the universal Church, and the consultation of an international theological forum by the Congregation for the Doctrine of the Faith. At no point, however, did these recommended reforms become truly effective.

It would be unrealistic to view the post-conciliar developments only in the negative light that is all too evident in some of them. If official policy has remained excessively reactionary in some areas, ecumenical developments at least have showed great promise. Vatican II inspired the official bilateral dialogues between Churches and communions that have flourished since 1965. On the international scene, the working of ARCIC-I (the Anglican Roman Catholic Internatioanl Conversations) was exemplary. Having been instructed by Pope Paul VI and Archbishop Ramsay to investigate the historical points of division between Anglicans and Catholics, ARCIC proceeded to do ecumenical theology in the best sense of the term. It systematically tried to arrive at joint positions on the neuralgic questions of the past, without using polemical terms or defending one-sided theologies that would doom any attempt at agreement. In their own spheres the international dialogues of the Catholic Church with the Lutheran World Federation and with the World Methodist Council did similarly fruitful work.

Here again the problem of reception that has affected the outcome of Vatican II could not be avoided. How are ecumenical agreements and agreed statements to be received? Paul VI, under whose inspiration these agreements were arrived at, had determined the initial step in the process of reception, namely, the publication of agreed statements with his explicit authorization and that of the archbishop of Canterbury, without, however, an official endorsement of their findings. This was all the more significant as similar authorizations had never been given before. Theologically, such publications implied a new attitude to doctrine. In the first place, the formulation of accepted doctrine could now result from a joint effort between members of Churches that are not in Eucharistic communion. In the second place, these formulations would normally become the object of public debate. The logical second step in the process of reception should have been, precisely, public evaluation.

When the *Final Report* of ARCIC-I was published in 1981, the process of reception required that bishops and theologians take their time to form a responsible opinion. But a wrench was thrown into the process by the immediate release of negative "observations" made by the Congregation for the Doctrine of the Faith. Henceforth the evaluation of the *Final Report* by national conferences of bishops was no longer reliable, since it was *de facto* guided by the negative position of the Roman dicastery in charge of watching over the faith.

This unfortunate episode contributed to the widespread impression that the leadership of the Catholic Church wished to undo some of the achievements of Vatican Council II. Such a drastic conclusion, however, ignores the inherent difficulties of reception. The reception of all previous ecumenical and general councils followed a curve that waved up and down. A down moment may last for decades. Given the two thousand years of the history of the Church, this should not cause surprise, discouragement, or depression. A down moment may prove to be more fruitful in the long run than the enthusiasm of an unreflecting up moment. The present down moment is marked above all by the dirth of candidate for the priesthood in the countries of Europe and the Americas. It is foreseeable that there soon will be so few active priests that the Catholic Church will be unable to function in the customary ways of the nineteenth and twentieth centuries. One may then envisage two scenarios. Either the hard-pressed bishops will ordain married men and also, presumably, women, to carry on the traditional Eucharistic ministry and pursue its pastoral implications. Or the laity will by necessity become the dominant agents in the transmission of the Christian faith to the next generations. And this cannot be without major effects on the administration of the sacraments. At the present time this must remain an open perspective.

CONCLUSION

LESSONS OF ECUMENISM

The previous reflections on the methodology of ecumenical dialogue are, I believe, as valid today as they were when they were composed. As it has taken place since Vatican II in bilateral and multilateral dialogues, and increasingly in personal research and reflection by a number of theologians, the encounter of Catholic thought with other traditions requires a rethinking of theological method, and it will lead to a revision of some formulations of doctrine. The necessity of this rethinking was sensed, somewhat confusedly, at Vatican Council II, when several of the conciliar documents initiated a restructuring of Catholic convictions. As the commissions and committees that wrote the texts made no systematic attempt to determine the form of such a restructuration, there resulted a series of rather disparate probes, toward liturgical theology (*Sacrosanctum concilium*), toward a reappropriation of neglected aspects of the ecclesiological tradition (*Lumen gentium*), toward a deeper experience of the Word of God in Scripture and in tradition (*Dei Verbum*), toward ecumenical thinking and practice (*Unitatis redintegratio, Nostra aetate*), toward an analysis of human existence in light of the signs of the times (*Gaudium et spes, Dignitatis humanae*). The trajectories of these probes intersected at two basic points. They turned away from the neo-scholasticism that prevailed in Catholic seminaries since Leo XIII. And they explored the insight of Paul VI that ecclesial life is radically dialogical. However, as they faced different partners in dialogue—the contemporary secular world, the religious traditions of Orthodoxy and of the Reformation, the religious beliefs, speculations, and experiences of non-Christian cultures, the positive aspects of post-Enlightenment political systems—they made no attempt at a mutual integration of their findings.

The notorious result of these probes was the post-conciliar explosion of new methodologies, as in transcendental Thomism, in liberation theology, in feminist theology, in African and Asian theologies that are still in the making, as also in the assumption that a pluralism of theologies should, in the long run, enhance the catholicity of the Church. These efforts initiated an ongoing reform. The first harvest of their fruits, however, was short-lived. The restructuration of the Roman Curia, that Pope Paul began, came short of the urgent demands of the situation. Paul VI, I believe, understood the necessity of far-reaching reforms in discipline and structure, but he was, for a number of reasons, unable to carry them out.

In regard to ecumenism the direction of thought of Vatican II's decree *Unitatis redintegratio* was progressively shaped by the initiatives of the Secretariat (Council) for the Unity of Christians. The ensuing bilateral dialogues contributed to a renewal of Catholic theology and doctrine, both at the level of method and at that of content. We are slowly, perhaps too slowly, learning to do theology ecumenically, in dialogue with other Christian traditions. Ecumenical theology goes beyond a comparison of the doctrines that have been diversely inherited from the past. After comparing the traditions it strives toward such a common understanding of the totality of Christian history that formerly diverging Christian strands may be able to appropriate some of the positions they rejected in the past. By appropriating I mean, not only that we learn from one another, but also that we recognize as our own what we would still consider alien if we worked in opposition to, or in isolation from, other Christians. This need not imply believing as true what was previously thought to be false. It means that in the process of dialogue one may be led to doubt, and eventually to abandon, conclusions that used to receive the note of certainty. Method and content, form and substance, are inseparable in theology. Fidelity to one method and its logic ensures that certain conclusions are reached. It is not accidental that medieval theology, diverse in its methods—as between monastic authors and scholastic professors, and between the several varieties of scholasticism—admitted a wide spectrum of positions, in regard, for instance, to exemplarism, theories of redemption, sacramental causality, Trinitarian analogies. Later, the theologies of the Counterreformation, as they narrowed their field to the interpretation of the great scholastics, came to accept less and less diversity in method and teaching.

Much more than the followers of other traditions have Catholics distinguished between theology, for which individual thinkers, writers, professors are ultimately responsible, and doctrine, which is officially determined and involves the agency of the College of bishops and of the bishop of Rome. Certainly doctrine has a theological basis, since issues cannot be thought out and debated without a grammar and a logic embedded in a language. Nonetheless, whether doctrine is taught topically in view of specific problems and questions, or magisterially as part of the apostolic deposit of faith, or formally proclaimed in a solemn definition, the relation of doctrine to its theological substratum and its contextual horizon should be loose enough for several theologies to be able to appropriate it.

A certain flexibility can be learned from the history of Christian thought. If the Nicaean confession, that the eternal Son is *homoousios* to the Father, is to be professed by all believers, it must be explainable and understandable in other languages than Greek, and in other forms and categories than those of Hellenistic culture. Likewise, describing the Eucharistic presence as transubstantiation, as was done at the council of Trent (session XIII, 1551[1]), should not be so tied to Thomism and its Aristotelian background that other theologies could not describe the real presence. Or also, the controversies of the Counterreformation on the *auxilia gratiae* should not make it impossible to acknowledge God's graciousness without dividing grace in actual and sanctifying, prevenient and concurrent, sufficient and efficacious, and even without affirming that we receive a gift called created grace.

Does the need to rethink theological method and conclusions extend to the content of doctrinal teaching? Undoubtedly, as new theological methods are tried, the form and the content of traditional teaching need to be recast. This may suggest that formulations of doctrine held to be normative—because endorsed by an ecumenical council, or proclaimed by the bishop of Rome speaking *ex cathedra*, or generally taught in all catechisms—will have to be reformulated. The perspective opened by such a question was precisely what concerned the Congregation for the Doctrine of the Faith when, in 1966, the *Dutch Catechism* presented Catholic doctrine in ways that were deemed to be incomplete or inaccurate. It was what intrigued the same dicastery about apparently new views in matters of sexual ethics. It also was what made it hesitant and dilatory in encouraging a favorable reception of the agreed statements of ecumenical commissions.

There undoubtedly are points of Catholic doctrine that ecumenical dialogues have shown to stand in the way of closer Christian unity. Such is the Counterreformation contention that the Roman Catholic Church is so identical with the Church of Christ that of all Churches and ecclesial communities it alone does not lack any essential element

1. *Enchiridion Symbolorum*, Denzinger-Schönmetzer, n.1642.

of the Church. Thus did Pius XII speak of the Catholic Church: "If we would define and describe this true Church of Jesus Christ, which is the One, Holy, Catholic and Apostolic Roman Church, we shall find nothing more noble, more sublime, or more divine than the expression, 'the Mystical Body of Jesus Christ'[2]." Again: "...the Mystical Body of Christ and the Roman Catholic Church are one and the same thing[3]." Logically, then, Pius XII even considered acknowledgment of the Roman primacy to be a condition of membership in the Church of God[4].

The formulation of Vatican II was more subtle: "The Church of Christ, constituted and ordered as a society in this world, subsists in the Roman Catholic Church[5]." The precise import of this formula is still debated. At the very least it shifts the primary focus of attention in ecclesiology. One should not think of the Church on earth, the community of salvation through Christ, primarily as it appears in its temporal and temporary aspects, or even as it must be by virtue of its essence, but rather in terms of its continuing subsistence as a society. Essence relates to the question, what is the Church? The answer is ontological. Subsistence relates to the question, where does the Church today experience its being? The answer is existential, for experience is an aspect of life. The expression, *subsistit in*, therefore, says that the Church of Christ is known to live and survive in the Catholic Church. However, the shift from ontology to experience raises a question that Vatican II did not attempt to answer: Does the Church of Christ also live, and thereby subsist, in other ecclesial institutions?

One is, at this point, at the cutting edge of an emerging ecclesiology. The ecumenical dialogues show that the Christians of other Churches and ecclesial communities are, as Vatican II recognized[6], closely related to the Church of Christ, not only in hope, but also in actual faith. The point is not that other Christians receive, as it were, a few crumbs falling from the Catholic table. Not only is it the case, as in an ecclesiology of *vestigia ecclesiae*, that they share "elements or goods,... many of which can

---

2. Encyclical *Mystici corporis*, 1943, n.13.

3. Encyclical *Humani generis*, 1950, n.27.

4. *Mystici corporis*, n.40.

5. *Lumen gentium*, n.6.

6. *Lumen gentium*, n.15.

exist outside the visible limits of the Catholic Church[7]." All Christian believers, in fact, have the experience of themselves sitting at the table of the Lord, even if they do not put the same stress on Eucharistic liturgy as Catholic theology does. The often raised, but largely obsolete question of the validity of sacraments concerns the recognition of external signs that testify to a sacrament being given. It says nothing about the actual gift and reception of sacramental grace. One should then agree with article IV of the Confession of Augsburg: The Church of Christ is to be found "where the grace of God is received by virtue of the word preached and of the sacraments administered according to the gospel."

Pope Paul VI opened a similar perspective when his analysis of the awareness of being the Church[8] led him to discern that the structure of ecclesial life is radically dialogical. The Church's self-awareness is itself inseparable from the experience of being the Church, and the awareness of being the Church is not found only in the Catholic context. All Christian believers share it as they gather in worship.

It is in the field of ecclesiology that ecumenical dialogues call for the greatest advances. If it is evident that all Christian communities, Orthodox, Catholic, or Protestant, do experience themselves as the Church, then one should logically acknowledge all Christian communities as being in some sense the Church. As soon as one perceives the life of Christ and the active presence of the Holy Spirit in communities that are not in communion with the bishop of Rome, the claim that these communities are in no sense the Church of Christ becomes a canonical fiction. The sense in which these communities are Church should be elicited from the specific characteristics of their awareness of being the Church. The result cannot be reduced to a matter of degree, as might be suggested by some lines of *Unitatis redintegratio* (n.13), where *ex parte* qualifies the "subsistence" of "Catholic traditions and structures" in the Anglican communion. One is not more or less the Church, just as one is not more or less saved by God through Christ. Rather, the Church continues in being within all Christian communities according to the measure of the grace of God, which is without measure. There will of course ensue certain implications regarding orders and ministry. In particular, the obsolescence of Leo XIII's judgment on Anglican ordinations in the apostolic letter *Apostolicae curae* (1896) ought to be

---

7. *Unitatis redintegratio*, n.3.

8. *Ecclesiam suam*, n.19-42.

acknowledged. Other implications could regard the relations between ecclesial communion and Eucharistic communion, the conditions for communion with the Catholic Church, and the rules for intercommunion.

What then, one may ask further, are the limits of the Church on earth? Paul VI looked beyond ecumenical dialogues when he located the Church in the "dialogue of salvation" that God has initiated with the world[9]. Since all peoples are involved in dialogue with God, they all have an intrinsic relationship to the Church of Christ. *Lumen gentium* describes this relationship briefly, yet positively enough to allow for a generous humanism in Catholic theology. Deeper reflection ought to follow regarding the ways in which the Holy Spirit is present and active in the religious traditions of all peoples. A wider ecumenism focused on the experience of God in all religions lies open to Catholic reflection.

---

9. *Ecclesiam suam*, n.74-79.

APPENDIX

CAN THEOLOGY BE NON-VERBAL?[1]

The question raised in this title may at first glance seem to be absurd. For the most obvious sense of the word, theology (from the Greek theos and logos), is, "talk" or "language about God." John Macquarrie modernized the translation as "God-talk." When the Gospel of John states, "The Word was made flesh," (John 1:14), we are not simply to understand that God's speech or communication system has become flesh. There is more to it than that. First, since the main insight behind the Johannine Logos theology derives from the Jewish concept of the *Dabar* of *Elohim*, which is deed as well as word, theology cannot be only God-talk. It must also, and at the same time, be God-deed, that is, not the actions of God, but human actions oriented to and motivated by God. Theology must be theopraxis. Second, Logos-theology acquired Greek connotations as soon as it was formulated in Greek, that is, in the gospel itself. Here, logos, at its most fundamental level, designates the inner rationality, the deep reason, that underlies both the appearance of the reality that humans experience, whether externally in the world or internally in their thoughts and feelings, and the proper use of language about that experience. Logos is the rationality of all that is, the intrinsic intelligibility of the universe. And since, in the Christian as in the Hebrew and Jewish perspective, God is the creator of all that is, then the inner rationality of God is present in the inner rationality of the universe. When therefore the Gospel of John says, "The Logos became flesh" (John 1:14), we are to understand that the inner rationality of the divine has now manifested itself in a totally new way, in the reality of flesh and blood of one human being, Jesus of Nazareth, whom Christians call Jesus Christ.

It follows that, whatever one may say about God in lectures and conversation, or to God in vocal prayer, speech is not the means of reaching the divine. In the formulation of John of the Cross, it is "faith" that is the only "proximate and proportional means" of union to God.[1] And

---

1. John Macquarrie, *God-talk*, New York: Harper and Row, 1967.

faith is not speech; it is an attitude of the mind and an orientation of the whole person. The creeds that formulate the agreed-upon beliefs of a given community are themselves neither faith nor means of union to God; they are criteria of membership in that community and pointers on the way to faith.

From the beginning of the Christian community, therefore, the disciples had to face two directions of theology. The verbal direction structures communication, thereby making community possible. The inner direction aims at some sort of perception of the rationality of the Creator and, through it, of the divine life. Insofar as the community comes first in experience, it was in the nature of things that verbal theology should emerge first. And thus the writings of the New Testament, whether letters or gospels or apocalyptic prophecy, were primarily destined to promote and strengthen the fledgling Christian communities. But their deeper dimension could not be hidden long. It came to the surface as a secondary reading of Scripture in the anagogical interpretation of its meaning. It was the mistake of the Gnostics that they made this reading primary.

When one looks at the Christian self-expression in the first five centuries of the Church, verbal theology is of course predominant in the patristic writings that have been preserved. But what I call nonverbal theology begins to take shape in the 3rd century, the clearest documentation for it lying in the catacombs, or underground cemeteries, of the city of Rome. Why did the Christians decorate their sarcophagi with sculptures, and the walls of their funeral chapels with frescoes? Of course they followed the practice of their contemporaries, who also had their own catacombs, both Jews of the Diaspora and adepts of the old Roman religion, which was, by that time, profoundly transformed by the "mysteries" of Greek, Egyptian and Persian origin. In the light of Logos-theology, however, the custom acquired a meaning that went beyond the requirements of a lingering cult of the dead. Motifs from the Old Testament, such as the crossing of the Red Sea, and from Roman paganism (thus, the image of the Good Shepherd) were given new meanings. The crossing of the Red Sea became the liberation from death by the Savior, itself symbolized by the victory of Emperor Constantine at the Milvius bridge. The Good Shepherd became Christ himself, his divinity carrying his humanity, according to the standard patristic interpretation of the scene. At one level, this was undoubtedly a pictorial way of expressing belief in the resurrection of the dead and the Incarnation of the Logos. But there was another level. As sculpture and painting are actions performed by artists and craftsmen, so contemplation of their work by those who visited the tombs of the martyrs and who participated in refrigeria (commemorative meals) entailed more than grasping a meaning. It implied entering into an action. The anonymous sculptor or painter opened a gate toward the creative and transforming act of God in Christ, so that the onlookers found themselves sharing the promise of the resurrection, assumed in the up building of "the body of Christ which is the Church," introduced into the divine life. St. Augustine may have missed this point when, in the Confessions, he bemoaned the fact that his mother, St. Monica, enjoyed attending these funerary rites!

The form that Greek Christianity gave this nonverbal theology has been best remembered. As it developed around Byzantium from the fifth century onwards, the art of the icons gave visual expression to a spiritual perception of the Christian mystery. As Church-buildings, rather than cemeteries, became the normal setting for this pictorial manifestation of the Christian faith, the spiritual focus passed from hope beyond death to the sacramental experience of Christian initiation. The Easter event is central: Christ rising from the dead "on the third day," breaking the gates of hell, pulling out Adam and Eve and the just of the Old Testament. Precisely, the Sunday liturgy is understood as a participation in the rising of Christ, though in the very life that is led on earth by the faithful. At the moment of the divine liturgy, the veil is lifted between earth and heaven. Likewise, in the icon the eyes of faith pass from the painting to its heavenly archetype, from the lines and colors showing Christ to Christ himself, from the New Testament scenes that are depicted to their ever-new rehearsal in the soul, from the Virgin theotokos to the God Incarnate whom she brought forth in his birthing, and whom she now presents to the faithful, from the saint that is depicted to the One from whom and by whom saints are.

The epic struggles of the 8th and 9th centuries between the iconodules and the iconoclasts (opposed to representing the divine in pictures) were more than rivalries between artistic movements. They were clashes between theologies. The iconoclasts admitted the sacrament of the Eucharist as the only nonverbal delineation of the divine presence that was acceptable in Christian orthodoxy. The iconodules maintained that, the Logos having become flesh, the whole of creation is now bathing in divine light—symbolically, the light of Mount Tabor at the transfiguration of Jesus -, being made translucent to the divine presence in the flesh. As St. John of the Cross expressed it later, in Spain, at the very time when El Greco, who was in part inspired by the icons, was painting in Toledo, "God works, and his work is God.[2]"

Thanks to Empress Irene, the art of the icons was saved by the II Council of Nicaea in 787. At the same time, their veneration was justified theologically: the worship offered to the type (the image) goes to the archetype. Under Empress Theodora, after another iconoclastic wave, the "triumph of orthodoxy" was confirmed with the restoration of the icons in 842 and 843. It was definitively assured at the IV Council of Constantinople, in 869-870. However, when the theologians of the Emperor of the Franks, Charlemagne, read the acts of Nicaea II in a faulty Latin translation, they reacted negatively. Icons, they thought, should be for education and edification, not for worship. Pictures or statues, however holy, have a catechetical, not a liturgical, purpose. At the Council of Frankfurt of 794 and in the Caroline Books that were then composed, the Frankish bishops took nonverbal communication through pictures as merely a substitute for verbal exchange. In spite of the endorsement of Nicaea II and the cult of icons and relics of saints by several popes, notably Pascal I (817-824), Hadrian II (867-872, who received Constantinople Council IV as ecumenical), and Gregory IV (827-844), who made the feast of All Saints universal and placed it on November 1, the Franks' understanding of holy pictures dominated Latin theology until the end of the Middle Ages. Formulated in the letters of Gregory the Great (pope, 590-604) to Serenus of Marseille, this restricted iconology was endorsed by Thomas Aquinas in his *Summa theologica* (II II, q. 94, a. 2, ad 12).

From that time on, Western Christian thought has been struggling between two positions. The one treats holy pictures as authentic means of spiritual ascent. The other downgrades their spiritual function to that of means of communication. The extreme form of this downgrading was reached when some of the Protestant movements abolished the use of pictures altogether. These opposite attitudes to icons are strictly parallel to opposite attitudes toward the living icons that the Orthodox and Catholics traditions call the saints. It was perhaps due to this tension that nonverbal theology practically vanished from consideration

---

2. *Subida del Monte Carmelo*, part II, ch. 9 (composed in 1578-1585): Simeon de la Sagrada Familia, ed., *Juan de la Ctruz. Obras completas*, 1972, p. 525.

in Latin Christianity, although it also remained alive and vibrant in at least two major movements of the medieval West.

The most obvious of these movements is still visible today for anyone who travels in Europe. It was the development of the Gothic art of the cathedrals, which of course was not limited to cathedrals, though, the cathedral being the Church of the bishop, central to a diocese, it was, and remains, more visible there. As may be seen in such a building as the cathedral of Chartres or, in a smaller scale, at the Sainte Chapelle in Paris, the Church building is a religious poem in stone, to which many arts and crafts contribute. The art of the architect delimits a structure in the air, with walls, pillars, arches, flying buttresses and vaults; it designs the façade and the successive orders of elevation of the building. The craft of the master mason gives solidity to the construction. The art of the sculptor extracts meaningful shape and religious sense from the stone, even in areas that remain invisible to pilgrims. The art of the painter—a feature that has mostly disappeared with the passing of time—imbues the walls with a coherent catechetical pattern: the Church is painted over most of its surface, showing scenes from the Old Testament, the Gospels (occasionally the Apocryphal Gospels), the Apocalypse, thus bringing to mind the historical past, the sacramental present, and the eschatological future, and thus inviting the faithful to participate in them. The art of the stained-glass maker and the glass painter fills the window space with a meaningful kaleidoscope of colors, which change with the varying clarity of the hours of each day, and fill the whole Church with a moving procession of lights. Over all this, the supreme art of the maître d'oeuvre or master builder unifies the project and ensures the harmonious collaboration of all.

In this setting the art of the singer will modulate the plain chant of the liturgy. The art of the dancer will, on certain occasions, act out the human search for God along the "labyrinth" on the floor of the Church (as at Chartres). The art of the homilist will bring life to the pulpit, which is set in the Church and sometimes alongside it, as at the cathedral of Medina del Campo, in Spain. All this is at the service of the sacramental art of the priest or bishop who celebrates the sacred mysteries at the main altar. In addition, the art of the actor will be engaged from time to time in liturgical or religious plays under the front portal, as at the York Minster. The art of the urban planner has set the cathedral on the central hill around which the city is built. In smaller village Churches, the art of the landscaper has designed and delimited God's acre around the Church, thus uniting the living and the dead in weekly and daily worship. At many points, of course, these nonverbal theologies interact with verbal theology. Preaching, plain chant, plays need speech. The overall design requires thought, and thought is formulated in words, that are also necessarily included in the writing of liturgical texts and the composition of theological tractates and *summae*.

From the standpoint of perspectival technique, the icon points to the divine by focusing on an imaginary point that stands either in front or behind the surface, but not on it, thus leading the onlooker within the self or beyond the appearances of the outside world and the literal meaning of the Scriptures that are illustrated. The miniature or illumination invites the attention to sharpen itself in order to delve into the infinitely small dimension of a micro-cosmos. In medieval imagination and spirituality, the model microcosmos is no other than the human body, in the proportions of which the entire created universe is reflected and, beyond and within the universe—in an intuition that should be related to the seven chakras of Hinduism, the Ogdoad of the Gnostics, and the Ten Sephiroth of the Kabbalah—the divine Trinity itself in its joint immanence and transcendence. The cathedral, into which one enters through the mystery that is depicted above the porch (often the scene of the final resurrection and the Last Judgment), urges the soul to enlarge itself. It is a macrocosmos that spiritually embraces the entire domain of creation, reaching to the ends of the earth at the four points of the compass, and joining earth to heaven in the ascending movement of its vaults and towers.

We have access to the second movement through the writings of the Christian mystics. In the proper theological sense of the term, mysticism, or mystical experience, or, as Teresa of Avila called it, "mystical theology," is, precisely, an experience of God that far escapes what can be said about it. Yet some mystics, led by the urgency of sharing their experience with others, have attempted to formulate it in words. But how has this been done? Taking the example of the one who is commonly recognized as the greatest mystical poet in Christendom, John of the Cross (1542-1591), we see that the primary expression of his experience is poetic[3], the explanation of the poetry, which comes later in his commentaries, being further removed from experiential immediacy. And though mystical poetry manifestly uses words and sentences, and uses them according to the recognizable grammar of the poet's language, it

3. *Dichos de luz y amor*, n. 106: *Obras*, p. 138.

is not objective. It does not express an ineffable experience through the descriptive power of what it says. It presents the reader with symbols. The proper way to read a symbol is not through an analytic investigation of what is said. One enters a symbol by reconstructing it. Its meaning can emerge only through a synthetic reshaping of the original experience. But such a reconstruction, though often attempted, is ultimately impossible. For the original experience was a gift (grace) that is never given again (though other gifts may be given); and in any case the experience of one person is never identical with that of another. It follows that the reading of mystical poetry must itself be nonverbal. The Spiritual Canticle of John of the Cross is truly read, neither when I pronounce the words of it, nor even when I understand the linguistic meaning of the lines, *Adonde te escondiste, / Amado, y me dejaste con gemido?* ("Where have you hidden, / Beloved, leaving me with my complaint?"), but when I am introduced to the meta-linguistic experience of God as my Lover and my Beloved, at the same time sensing God's infinite distance from myself. This infinite distance may be, and has been, diversely experienced at the four transcendental levels of divine Being, Oneness, Goodness, and Beauty. Faced with the divine Being, my 'I' has no being (*nada*), it is lost in multiplicity, it is steeped in impiety, it is ugliness itself. And yet, insofar as God carries me into the divine life, then I know by experience, with John of the Cross, that I am also "God by participation,[4]" that I am beautiful with God's Beauty, as God is beautiful with my beauty[5].

I have tried to show that there is an important basis in the Catholic tradition for attempts to express theology through architecture, painting, ritual, art, music, and dance. At its deepest level, the experience of God is nonverbal. Verbal theology is the paradoxical effort to understand and explain the experience of God in the context of a given community of belief. It is paradoxical, because only indirectly can words lead into the metalinguistic realm. It may learn from the symbolic paths which, in all religions, have been followed by pilgrims in search of the divine. Through the divine dimension imprinted upon the universe by

---

4. See my book, *Poetry and Contemplation in St. John of the Cross*, Athens, OH: Ohio University Press, 1988.

5. *Cantico*, st. 38, n. 3: *Obras*, p. 401.

Creation the Absolute reaches down to us, contingent creatures, and introduces us into the realm of the divine glory. The Christian tradition has couched this faith in Trinitarian terms. The one and only God has been experienced as the Logos and the Spirit who jointly lead to the eternal Father.

As a practitioner of verbal theology, I have used thousands of words in speeches and in books. As a priest I have practiced the liturgical ritual of the Catholic Church, which I have found to be truly sacramental: a sacrament is a symbol that effectively brings the faithful into communion with what it points to. I have also expressed religious and theological insights through the medium of poetry, both in English and in French. I have received the kiss of divine grace in the contemplation of painting and sculpture. And it is with awe and gratitude that I also try to learn from the arts that are beyond my capacities.

INDEX